FROM PRAM

TO PRIMARY SCHOOL

Parenting small children
from birth to age six or seven

by Michael and Terri Quinn

Family Caring Trust

First published 1995
by Family Caring Trust,
44 Rathfriland Road
Newry
Co. Down
BT34 1LD
Tel. 028-3026-4174
Fax. 028-3026-9077
(From Rep. of Ireland replace 028 with 048)
Website: familycaring.co.uk
e-mail: office@familycaring.co.uk

Illustrations and design: Pauline McGrath
Printing: W&G Baird Ltd

Reprinted (with minor revisions each time)
1996, 1997, 1998 (twice) 1999, 2000, 2001, 2002, 2003, 2004 (twice), 2005, 2006, 2007,
2008, 2009, 2010, 2011, 2012, 2014

ISBN 978-1-872253-10-7

CONTENTS

Before You Begin   5

Chapter 1: Behaviour You Don't Like   8

Chapter 2: Encouraging Your Child   16

Chapter 3: Listening Means Paying Attention   24

Chapter 4: Talking With Your Child   33

Chapter 5: Discipline   41

Chapter 6: Quality Time   50

Appendix: Your Child's Spiritual Development   58

Further Reading   67

Agreements   69

CHILDREN HAVE RIGHTS

The UN Convention on the Rights of the Child is the first document to attempt to write down all the rights of children up to 18 years. Here are some highlights. It may help to think of these rights as basic needs – try replacing 'right to' with 'need (for).'

1. **Children have a right to be respected by their parents or guardians, and to be involved in decisions that affect themselves.**
2. **Children have a right to say what they want and think and feel so long as doing so does not break the law or affect other people's rights.**
3. **Children have a right to personal privacy, including not having personal letters opened or phone calls listened to unless the law allows this.**
4. **Children have a right to a wide range of information, especially any which would make life better for them.**
5. **Children have a right to proper care and protection from all forms of violence, including cruel punishment, belittling, or lack of respect.**
6. **Children have a right to an adequate standard of living, good food, good health care, and the best possible chance to develop fully.**
7. **Children with a disability have a right to be enabled to take an active, full part in everyday life and become as independent as possible.**
8. **Every child is entitled to rest and play, and to have the chance to join in a wide range of activities.**

...AND PARENTS HAVE RIGHTS

1. **Parents have the same right to be listened to and respected by their children as their children have to be listened to and respected by their parents.**
2. **Parents have a right to time for relaxing and developing themselves – also a right to time on their own with a spouse or other significant adult.**
3. **Parents have a right to postpone making a decision until they have had time to think.**
4. **Parents have a right to say 'no,' to set reasonable limits for their children, and, within reason, to let them experience the effects of ignoring those limits.**
5. **Parents have a right to have their work at home valued and appreciated by the significant people in their lives as well as by government and state bodies.**
6. **Parents have the right to ask their children for reasonable help around the home, according to each child's ability.**
7. **Parents have a right to communicate their values and opinions to their children – though they cannot force their children to have the same values.**
8. **Parents have a right to proper support in providing their children with due rights and respect.**

Do you agree that you and your children have these rights? Which of your children's rights might you find hardest to respect? Which of your own rights might you find hardest to claim?

BEFORE YOU BEGIN

Observing people in pairs

Have you ever watched an adult with a child, and then two adults together, in a public place? Did you notice a difference? Recently, Valerie Yule looked at people in streets, buses and shops. She wanted to see how people in pairs got on together, so she looked at each pair for three minutes. She found that the 85 pairs of adults she watched were reasonably courteous to each other – they spoke together, or at least smiled or looked at each other, except in a few cases. But she found that pairs of an adult and a child were different. In 65 of the 85 pairs she watched, there was no communication (even looking) between the adult and the child in the first two minutes she watched them. When there was communication, it was mostly negative – 'Don't,' 'No,' smacks, commands to behave, scolding, pulling by the arm, fixing clothes without speaking, giving a sweet to a crying child who had just been cuffed, ignoring a child who was speaking, telling a child to be quiet.

Valerie described this as adult 'rudeness' to children. But she was also aware that the blank, numb expression she saw on many of the parents' faces was telling its own story of pain and misery.

Many parents are suffering as well as their children. Many of us know that what we are doing is wrong, but we may feel helpless to change.

Change is possible!

People like family therapist Virginia Satir have shown that, no matter how bad things may seem in your family, change is always possible. Over the past twenty-five years, too, many new possibilities have been emerging for families.

Even in the past ten years, we have seen many thousands of parents change as a result of doing courses in effective parenting. These parents were often surprised to find themselves communicating better with their children and enjoying them more. We hope that will be your experience too as you work through this course.

A little at a time

This is the handbook for a 7-week programme (8 weeks if you wish to include the optional session on spiritual development). There is also a leader's guide and a 90-minute dvd. Parents tend to find the book or dvd helpful without a course (and a useful way to get partners and family on their wavelength), but these tools are best used in a small group of parents. If you are working through the book on your own, you may find it more useful to read just a chapter at a time, as parents following a course would do.

If you would like to belong to a group, you may like to contact your school, PTA, or church – or a local organisation that supports parents. Family Caring Trust provides resources and support to thousands of such groups.

Who is it for?

This book is for parents of children aged up to six or seven – or eight! ('Parent' here may mean father, mother, adoptive parent, step-parent, guardian, foster-parent, child minder, teacher – anybody working with or caring for children.) It is for ordinary parents, including those who are single or separated, those whose children have special needs, or whose families are broken or mixed, as well as those who are married. It is aimed at men as well as women, encouraging *fathers* to be more involved in parenting and in *co*-parenting.

Some ideas in the book will not apply to babies up to a year old, but then it often helps to look at issues before they are on top of you – that may even give you a few months' head start!

Language

The book is written in simple language, without jargon, but some words we use may cause you difficulty. 'Parenting' is not a word everyone likes, but it is preferable to 'mothering' or 'fathering' with their sexist overtones. Some of you may dislike the word 'misbehaviour,' but it will be clear that we do not see misbehaviour as something a child does on *purpose*; we prefer to use a well-known word like 'misbehaviour' than to continually repeat a phrase like 'unacceptable behaviour.'

We speak of a child sometimes as 'he,' but more often as 'she' – to help right the balance.

Using what works for you.

The suggestions in this book are meant to *help* you, not to make you feel worse. We are all doing our best in what is often a thankless, frustrating, and exhausting task. Feel free to disagree with anything in these pages that does not suit you. Use what works for you. After all, each of us is different. Our family backgrounds are different. Each child is different. There is no one way to bring up children. Much depends on your circumstances, on the position of a child in your family – even on your mood. It would be foolish not to listen to experts, but it is not helpful to let experts dictate to you or tell you how to bring up your children. We hope the book will help you to figure out some things you *could* do in raising your children, not tell you what you *should* do.

each of us is different

Beliefs and influences

Our goal in writing this book is to help provide some relief from the isolation and confusion you may experience, and to foster respect between you and your child. We want to help you create a situation in which your children can learn to love themselves and others, become responsible, and develop their fullest potential. Our aim is not to change or modify children's behaviour to come up to some kind of ideal or model. Each child is unique and special, and part of our task is to *encourage* this creativity and uniqueness.

Many good ideas that could have been included have been left out in order to keep the book simple. The emphasis is on learning *skills* rather than giving you information, as there are already good, simply written resources (like the Open University materials) on child psychology and the development of children. Besides, charts of children's development can be misleading without some expert guidance, as children develop at such different rates.

Some simple psychological ideas have been introduced, mainly those of Alfred Adler, as developed by Dreikurs, Dinkmeyer and McKay (notably natural and logical consequences, and the goals of misbehaviour). On the other hand, there is little emphasis here on skills for negotiating and solving problems, as these are dealt with in our books for parents of children over five.

The ideas in the book are not original. We also owe a great deal to the work and thinking of John Bowlby, Dolores Curran,

Rudolf Dreikurs, Gerard Egan, Erik Erikson, Thomas Gordon, Patty Wipfler, Carl Rogers, Virginia Satir, and Donald Winnicott. Some of the icebreakers for the programme have been adapted from "Playing with fire; Training for the creative use of conflict." by Nic Fine and Fiona Macbeth, Publ. Youth Work Press, 1992.

We would like to thank the people whom we consulted at different stages about style and content, and those who helped test the programme in Britain and Ireland – Helen Albans, Gabrielle Allman, Pauline Bree, Heather Byrne, Anne Coughlan, Jane Crouch, Audrey Dillon, Joan Ellis-Jones, Regina Gallagher, Joan Gollogly, David Gamble, Lynda Irwin, Tim Kahn, Jill Lance, Naomi and John Lederach, Philip Leonard, Elizabeth McAllister, Catherine and Michael Molloy, and Lori Shearer – and a great many parents whose openness to experiencing the course and whose honest reactions to the book kept changing its shape throughout the different stages of piloting. Thanks, too, to our youngest children, Colm and Ruth, without whom the book would have lacked some of its practicality.

CHAPTER 1: BEHAVIOUR YOU DON'T LIKE

Edward: Mummy!

Mother: You're not out of bed again!

Edward: But mummy...

Mother: Back to bed! No excuses!

Edward: Mum-mee!!

Mother: What is it!

Edward: I can't sleep.

Mother: Well, you'd *better* sleep! I've had enough of this! Come on – back up the stairs!

Edward: But mummy!... I'm thirsty...

Mother: You've had a drink.

Edward: Only a little drink. I'm thirsty again...

Mother: Okay, then, but this is your last drink. You understand?...

Three-year-old Edward did understand. He understood *very well* how to keep his mother busy with him. He got up three more times that evening, once to go to the toilet (which took about five minutes), once (briefly) to say he "still couldn't sleep," and finally (for 25 minutes) to "see who had come in" and be made much of by the visitor!

Like puppets on a string

Why is Edward doing this? Why is he demanding so much attention? Why does this power-struggle develop each evening at bedtime?

Isn't it partly because of the way Edward's mother is dealing with the situation? She is doing her best to be a good parent, but Edward probably knows exactly what she is going to do or say. Like many children, he has learnt how to control and get attention from his parents (though he does not do this consciously). Children can often keep their parents going like puppets on a string, getting them to scold, plead, threaten, bribe – and often give in. **They learn exactly what 'bait' to use to 'hook' their parents into dealing with their problems or squabbles, and they have discovered that parents often do exactly what their children *expect* them to do.**

Come on! Back up the stairs!

But before we look at how parents can be more effective, it may help to ask what is going on in the child's mind.

Why is my child behaving like this?
Much behaviour you do not like may not be misbehaviour at all. Crying, for example, particularly in the first year of life, may simply be children's way of communicating that they are wet or hungry or tired or sore or lonely. Or what seems like misbehaviour may simply be normal curiosity (like playing with coal) or inexperience (like spilling orange juice).

Misbehaviour normally only occurs when children are *discouraged* or feel *bad* about themselves; it is not something they do on purpose. In the first few years of their life they have so much to learn that, when they fail to achieve something, or when a need is not being met, they look for your attention in the only way they know – they express their fears, loneliness or discouragement in 'troublesome' behaviour. Misbehaviour is their cry for help. It says, "Look, I'm out of control. I can't cope. I don't know what to do next. I need some security."

It would be nice if a child could *tell* you what the matter was. Even if she has the words, however, she usually doesn't even *know* what is going on for her. A behaviour you don't like becomes her way of getting your attention. And it works. It doesn't matter that your attention is negative – nagging, shouting, even smacking. That feels better than no attention at all.

Four common ways of misbehaving
Here are four common ways in which children misbehave:

1. Attention seeking – keeping you busy with them. They will refuse to eat, or start squabbling – probably not even *aware* that they are seeking attention.

2. Power contests – refusing to eat or to settle in bed at night may be a way of testing to find out what limits there are.

3. Revenge seeking. If you constantly 'win' and your children 'lose,' they may seek ways of getting even with you – perhaps a pouting "Go away. I hate you," as you are about to give a hug! Revenge seeking can occur from about 18 months onwards.

4. Showing inadequacy. Very discouraged children may believe they are incapable of learning to swim, or to cycle, or to button their buttons, or whatever, and they may then refuse even to *try*. As a

They will refuse to eat

result, they often get extra attention – and find that more is done for them! Showing inadequacy will not normally occur until a child is three years old – and usually only after some months of feeling discouraged.

How parents react in turn
As parents, we often react to misbehaviour in fixed, unthinking ways – perhaps as *our* parents or guardians used to react. That is the only model most of us have had. And the amazing thing psychologists have noticed is that **the way we react usually *rewards* the misbehaviour instead of correcting it! We reward misbehaviour by paying attention to it.** When we give attention on demand to the child who won't eat, or to children squabbling, we may be guaranteeing that the behaviour will continue. When we look for a lost sock for the child who shows inadequacy, or when we take over the tying of their shoes, aren't we similarly rewarding the 'inadequacy' and ensuring that the behaviour will continue? Let's look in more detail at an example of how parents often react.

Permissive and authoritarian reactions
Two-year-old Milly had learnt to feed herself, but has gone backwards since her baby sister was born. How do her parents react? Milly's mother is now so anxious about Milly not eating that she spends more time coaxing her – and offers her biscuits and sweets between meals. Milly is keeping her mother busy, being rewarded for not eating, and getting lots of extra attention. Milly's father is unhappy about what is happening. "She has to eat proper food!" he says, "What you're doing is only spoiling her!" But his 'solution' is even worse. He decides to force the spoon into Milly's mouth. A power struggle develops. Milly resists, spits out the food, and her father gets angry and smacks her. Eventually, he seems to win – or rather, he wins the battle but loses the war when she gets her revenge by rejecting him, "Me don't like Daddy!" In all this, she is the centre of attention, and getting lots of notice!

"Want a nanna now!"

Can you see what is happening? **Neither the permissive/ bribing approach *nor* the no-choices/ punishing approach is effective in the long term.** Both play into the child's hands, giving her extra attention and reinforcing her mistaken idea that misbehaviour is the only way to get your attention.

A more effective approach

So what can a parent do? What is an effective and respectful approach? Let's see what happened when Milly's parents, as a result of this course, backed off and took a fresh approach. When Milly refused to eat breakfast, her father said:

"That's okay, Milly. You don't have to eat it."

Milly was surprised and puzzled. She was not getting the extra attention she had expected. Besides, you can't have a power struggle with someone who doesn't fight back! But she kept testing.

"Want a nanna! [banana]"

"You can have a banana for lunch," her mother said.

"Want a nanna now!" Milly said.

Mum and Dad stayed as calm as possible, but they didn't budge. Milly cried, then screamed, in the hope of changing them, but her screaming wasn't rewarded as before. More tears and screams followed when Mum refused to give her anything to eat between meals. Interestingly, Mum did not say 'no.' Instead, she spoke positively and

respectfully, "Yes, you can have something nice to eat at lunch-time."

Within a few days, the problem was solved. Not only was Milly eating much better, but she was also *happier* (as children often are when they know what the limits are).

No instant solutions

There is no magic in dealing with misbehaviour. There are no easy, instant solutions. Each child is different. Each parent is different. You have different histories and backgrounds, different personalities and circumstances. A suggestion, however, is that you **stop *rewarding* misbehaviour, give less attention to it, perhaps take a new and different approach instead – even do the *opposite* to what you normally do.** Instead of attempting to sort out the squabbles, you might simply refuse to take sides (unless there is real danger), "I trust you to sort this out on your own." When you find yourself in an argument or power-struggle with your child, try backing off and see if you can *postpone* dealing with the behaviour instead of letting yourself get sucked in. When your children want a decision *now*, say you need time to think about it. Try ignoring attention-seeking behaviour – like a child using swear words – and see how much more powerful your silence can be. Children (like adults!) hate to be ignored. But don't let your silence become *sulking* – do keep a sense of humour!

"It doesn't work for me!"

There is no guarantee that taking a new approach will work for you. Indeed, two families will sometimes find that completely *opposite* approaches work for them. Sometimes, too, you may need to experiment with a number of approaches before you find one that suits you – though you will probably need to persist with one for a week or two before you decide it is not for you. Let's look again at the example of a child not settling at bedtime and see why it is that taking a new approach will not always be effective initially.

Like Edward in the first example, four-year-old Alice was very good at keeping her mother, Liz, busy with her after being settled for the night. Liz, a single parent, felt bad about leaving Alice with a child-minder all day. When she had read Alice a story, Alice wanted another and another. Then Alice 'couldn't sleep' unless Liz got in beside her. An hour later, Liz was still lying beside her, feeling terribly frustrated – and Alice was still awake! Liz's whole evening was taken up with this bedtime routine. On doing the parenting course, Liz decided on a new, firmer approach. She read Alice one story, and then announced:

"Now, darling, I want you to go to sleep, and I don't want you to get up any more. Okay?"

Alice wanted another story and another

It did not work, for Alice knew she was still in control. She knew it from Liz's sweet smile and less-than-confident tone of voice. Liz's *words* may have been firmer, but Alice could hear her mother's apology *through* them. She knew she still had her mother around her little finger, and she continued to find excuses for stretching out the bedtime routine for hours. Only when Liz stopped apologising and *acted* did a change come about:

"If you get up again, Alice, I'll put you to bed earlier tomorrow evening."

This was not an empty threat. In spite of Alice's tears (and Liz's guilty feelings),

Alice was in bed ten minutes earlier the next evening – and aware that she would also be in bed early the following evening if she got up again. Within a week, Liz could not believe the change. There was peace in the evening, she had time for herself – and Alice was actually more content!

Change, then, may not come immediately, but trying a new approach can help you to be more effective – withdrawing from power struggles, giving less attention to misbehaviour, when possible, acting instead of talking, and giving positive attention when it is not being expected.

"I no longer felt so exhausted."
This idea of trying a new approach is well illustrated by a health visitor, herself a parent, writing in the English Health Visitors' magazine shortly after doing the Family Caring Trust course. She wrote:

I had normally shouted, so I resolved to be quieter. I refused to give attention on demand and I decided to back off when I found myself getting hooked into an argument or a fight. I ignored fighting and squabbling unless there was real danger. In this way, I began to change unthinking patterns of parenting that were not effective, and I was no longer rewarding misbehaviour. I began to spend more time giving positive attention to the children."

"What a difference this all made to me. I started to unwind. I no longer shouted in the morning, and the house became quieter. And I no longer felt so exhausted from continually running after the children."

Looking after yourself
The last comment above seems important: another way of doing the opposite to what you normally do may be to look after *yourself*. **If you do not deal with the anger and stresses and tensions in your own life, it is easy to take them out on a child.** Children do not need stressed parents.

Maybe a first step is to settle for being a less than perfect parent and to say 'no' to guilt. You cannot do all you would like to do. It may help to decide what is essential and what can be left out or postponed. Ask for help when you need it – even something obvious like taking turns with another parent in minding each other's children so you can get out. You need to get out. You need some exercise and fresh air. You also need time on your own, preferably up to half an hour a day in a bath or with your feet off the ground, listening to your own kind of music, reading, focusing on your breathing, or doing whatever it is that relaxes you. And you need to meet other adults, particularly if you are a single parent.

If you are a couple, all the extra demands of small children may leave either or both of you stressed and impatient, with less energy for each other. A woman may have many of her needs for touch and cuddles met by a baby – while her partner buries himself in extra work, perhaps not even aware of his feelings of loneliness and jealousy. Maybe you need a weekly 'date' – perhaps just getting out together for a walk. You may find your child also becomes happier as a result.

In the planning session at the end of this chapter there are a number of ways of dealing with stress. You may like to choose a few that appeal to you.

See what misbehaviours you can ignore.

Summing up

To sum up, then. Children love to be noticed: they need and want your attention. From about one year old, they will often begin to misbehave, keeping you busy with

them or trying to control things. This is not conscious or deliberate – they just discover that misbehaviour is 'noticed' and gets them extra attention – and they prefer scolding or even smacking to no attention at all. **So parents are actually *rewarding* misbehaviour and causing it to *increase* by paying so much attention to it.**

One effective way of dealing with misbehaviour, then, is to give *less* attention to it, when possible – to cut right back on nagging, scolding, arguing, sorting out squabbles, etc. – but to give *more* attention to your children when they are *not* expecting or demanding it. **Misbehaviour usually needs an audience, and you are no longer providing an audience when you are silent or when you turn your attention away.** See what misbehaviours you can ignore, then – no talking, no looking, no touching – except perhaps to prevent children from hurting themselves or others. If possible, you might even leave the room. Parents tend to under-use the powerful tool of silence.

This does not mean accepting misbehaviour and doing nothing about it. Children who are troubled and misbehaving need their carers to rescue them from the dead end they have got into. Limits need to be set around their misbehaviour. In a later chapter we will be looking at effective ways of setting limits. You are already becoming effective, however, if you take away attention from misbehaviour and give good attention when it is *not* being demanded. You are providing your children with the affection and encouragement they need, and you are no longer rewarding their misbehaviour.

up to half an hour a day in the bath

TABLE 1: AVOIDING THE BAIT*

Discouraged children will often seek mistaken goals - though they are not consciously laying bait to hook you in. Parents often take the bait and may actually reward the child's behaviour; especially by giving attention on demand. The suggestions below, for "avoiding the bait" may not suit you, but can you see how you might be more effective if you took a different approach?

MISBEHAVIOUR (BAIT IS LAID) Not deliberate - child is usually discouraged.	PARENT SEES BAIT/ MISBEHAVIOUR Your feelings are often a clue to child's goal.	..AND GETS HOOKED (AUTHORITARIAN) Authoritarian parent may actually reward behaviour	...OR GETS HOOKED (PERMISSIVE) Permissive approach may also reward misbehaviour.	...OR AVOIDS BAIT (EFFECTIVE) Possible ways to "unhook" and take new approach.
Example 1. Three-year-old and one and a half-year-old constantly fighting and squabbling.	Parent feels **ANNOYED**. (Your annoyance is often a clue that your child is seeking **ATTENTION**.)	Mum scolds, threatens, etc. Children prefer this negative attention to no attention at all.	or Mum pleads, moans, reasons with them - which also gives the children attention on demand.	or She ignores squabbling unless there is danger - or she simply offers a choice - to separate or co-operate.
2. Two-year-old Darren cries when put to bed. It takes hours to settle him - it has become a battle of wills.	Parent feels **ANGRY**. (Your anger is often a clue that you and your child are in a **POWER** struggle.)	Dad is drawn into power struggle - eventually loses temper, shouts, and dumps Darren, screaming, in bed.	or Dad gets into bed along with Darren. An hour later, Dad lets him stay up.	or He prepares for bedtime with quietening time and story. Dad ignores crying, stays firm but friendly.
3. Four-year-old Zoe didn't get her own way. Later, she throws a tantrum in front of Mum's visitor.	Parent feels **HURT**. (Your hurt feelings are often a clue that child is seeking **REVENGE**.)	Mum gives Zoe an angry spanking, but Zoe becomes defiant and is even worse next time.	or Mum stores up future problems by "soothing" Zoe, "There, there, now," and offering her a sweet.	or Mum carries Zoe off to have tantrum in bedroom or Mum leaves room - but gives good attention later.
4. Five-year-old Paul refuses to learn to ride his bicycle, - frightened of falling off and convinced he cannot learn.	Parent feels **HELPLESS**. (Your helpless feeling is often a clue that child is showing **INADEQUACY**)	Dad reinforces inadequacy by forcing Paul around on bike, and, when Paul doesn't improve, saying, "He's just plain lazy!"	or Dad coaxes, bribes, and reasons with Paul (giving lots of attention to the "problem") - all to no avail.	or Attention taken off cycling and encouragement given in areas he is good at. He grows in confidence and learns to cycle later.

*This table is based on the discoveries of Alfred Adler, as developed by Rudolf Dreikurs; Don Dinkmeyer and Gary McKay. The "bait" idea comes from Dolores Curran.

GETTING IN TOUCH

*Put the first letter of your child's name beside anything in the list below you sometimes have to deal with. Then mark **one** area where you would like to be more effective (not something big – it is usually better to start with something small and get a sense of success or progress):*

Baby crying a lot.
Baby crying at bedtime.
Won't let you change nappy.
Toddler making a scene at bath time or bedtime.
Not staying in bed.
Constant whinging throughout the day.
✓ Very messy with food.
Taking biscuits without permission.
Noisy play.
Biting.
Spitting at people.
Not saying 'hello' to friends who visit.
Hitting someone with a stick, fist or hand.
Using swear words.
Eating soil/ sand.
Soiling or wetting – just when toilet trained.
Constant squabbling with friend, sister or brother.
✓ Making a scene to get out of high chair and sit on parent's lap at dinnertime.
Running across the street alone
✓ Putting hands into food.
Disruptive at play-school.
Dangerous climbing on furniture or walls.
Toys, crayons, books left scattered on floor.
Temper tantrums.
Battles over dressing.
Keeps you awake at night.
Won't co-operate unless you offer a treat.
Won't eat.
Gets into parents' bed during night.
Answers back.
Says 'no' to everything.
Interrupts you when you have visitors.
Does almost everything (s)he's told not to do.
Won't share toys.
Refuses to wear a coat going out.
Something else?..

CASE STUDIES

A. There is constant fighting and squabbling between 3-year-old Ann and 4-year old Tony. Ann often starts it – teasing and taunting her brother until he pulls her hair. When she screams, mum comes running and gets involved in 'refereeing' the dispute. Mum usually takes Ann's side, scolding Tony and accusing him of bullying. She makes empty threats about what will happen if there is more fighting.

a. How is the mother not being effective?
b. Which of the following ideas might be more effective instead? (Please respect those who disagree with you.)

1. Just *observe* what is going on, making no comment, remaining silent.
2. Ask them to come back in a minute and tell you what they're going to do about it.
3. Just ignore the squabbling unless there is serious abuse or violence.
4. Remove the disputed toy until they agree whose turn it is.
5. Ask them to leave the room until they make up.
6. Separate them, and perhaps talk it out later, when things are calmer.
7. Another suggestion?

B. Five-year-old Celia regularly gets into her parents' bed during the night, saying her bed is cold. Mum moans but is too tired to do anything, and then sleeps poorly. Dad, if he awakens, is cross with her, and carries her back to bed. She often returns later, and climbs in at Mum's side.

a. How are the parents not being effective, even rewarding the nightly disturbances?
b. Which of the following ideas might be more effective instead?

1. Give her an alarm clock and tell her not to come in until it rings.
2. Mum decides to carry her back to her bed.
3. Welcome her in and let her sleep with you.
4. Say, "If you get out of your bed tonight, you'll have to make up for your loss of sleep by going to bed earlier tomorrow." And mean it.
5. Give her a hot water bottle instead.
6. Another suggestion?

SKILL PRACTICE

*How did your parents or guardians deal with misbehaviour when you were a child? – did they shout, or smack, or plead, or nag, or moan, or get impatient, or what?... Can you see ways in which that has influenced you in how **you** deal with misbehaviour today – either in **similar** ways to them or in **reacting** to their methods by doing the opposite?*

PLANNING

1. Ways of dealing with stress

*Change begins with yourself, so one thing you could do differently this week is to look **after** yourself. Which of the things in the next column might help you cope better, especially when you are stressed? Put a tick beside anything you'd like to try; then decide which of the suggestions you have ticked you will try first. When? Where? You may like to write down specifically what you plan to do.*

2. If you have a partner...

If you have a partner who is not doing the course, or if a parent or other adult is living in your home, try to get their backing and to involve them – for example by sharing this book or the video, and by talking through the ideas with them.

3. A new approach

*How will you deal differently with **one** misbehaviour this week? Perhaps the behaviour you marked in the 'Getting in touch' section. Be specific – with which child? When? Where? What exactly will you do or say – or not do, or not say? You may like to write your plans.*

• Say to yourself something like: *"Relax," "Calm down,"* or *"I'm okay."*
• If you can't have time alone now, plan a hot bath or some treat later.
• When you're annoyed, leave the room, or count to ten before you act.
• Ask someone for help – even a short break so you can take a rest.
• Get outside into the fresh air for a walk – even *with* the children.
• Go and *scream* where the children can't hear you, if that's possible – or thump a pillow or cushion.
• Sit down, close your eyes and think of a peaceful scene for a few minutes.
• Get out regularly with one or two friends – even talk on a phone.
• Relax with feet off the ground, and breathe more deeply and slowly.
• If you are a couple, plan a 'date' for one evening a week.
• Ring a Parent line – look in the directory under 'Parent.'
• Say 'no' to guilt by doing something you enjoy – swim, read, walk...
• Find skilled help before things get worse, especially if you're abusing your child.
• Another way to care for yourself?...

My plans _____

_____

• Please read chapter two of your handbook before the next session.

CHAPTER 2: ENCOURAGING YOUR CHILD

*'No! Don't touch that! Mummy says **no**! Did you hear me? I said **no**! Now put that back! And don't think I'm not watching you! How many times do I have to tell you to stop making a mess!... I said **stop** it! Just **stop** it! Do it again and you'll get a smack where it hurts. Now I've warned you! You're becoming very, very spoilt, and you're not going to get away with it any more! Do you hear!!..."*

The effects of nagging and scolding

Do you know how many times, on average, a parent nags or scolds a pre-school child every day? Fifty five times, according to a recent study. There are all kinds of reasons why this happens, including the fact that the child who most needs love often makes herself the most difficult to love. But can you imagine the effect on children of this constant nagging, reminding, scolding, shouting, and fault finding, often delivered in an impatient, angry, disrespectful tone of voice? You will tend to come across as a negative rather than a positive person in the eyes of your child, and you will tend to breed resentment, anger and constant power-struggles. Many two-year-olds' favourite word is 'no,' perhaps because they have heard 'no' more than any other word.

In chapter one, we saw how ineffective this constant attention to misbehaviour is. Negative attention is not only ineffective, however; but it also does damage. When parents have to shout and smack *more* to get the same effect, it can more easily happen that they drift into causing physical or emotional abuse. **Constant criticism also undermines children's *confidence*. They develop guilt, shame and low self-esteem. They often end up believing the negative things that are said in anger by someone they love** – that they are bad, cheeky, stupid, naughty, disgusting, or worse. Many adults still go around today believing and being affected by wrong messages like these, which they picked up when they were small.

they've heard 'no' more than any other word

"I'll misbehave less if you notice me..."

What may be just as serious as paying attention to misbehaviour is the *lack* of attention we pay to what is *positive and good* in our children. We notice children when they are squabbling, but we can easily ignore them when they are playing quietly. We sometimes make a bigger fuss when they wet their pants than when they make steady progress in potty training. Some parents only sing to children who are crying or who will not sleep. Some only play with a child when they feel they have no choice.

Positive attention often stops when children come into their second or third year. They may then begin to misbehave in an attempt to be noticed, since they are not noticed otherwise! If they had words to express themselves, they might say something like:

"Mummy..., Dad..., you were so lovely to me in the first year of my life. I knew you loved me and I felt great security, because you looked after all my needs with such attention. I felt precious and secure.

What has happened? I miss your smiles and cuddles and all the lovely things you used to say to me. Why don't you notice me much now? Aren't you pleased to see me develop and grow and make my own decisions? Have I done something wrong? Am I bad? Don't you love me any more?

When I couldn't talk, you used to listen

with big round eyes. When I couldn't walk, you paid such good attention and encouraged every little step. Now you don't seem very interested. I know I misbehave a lot now, but it seems to be the only way I get your attention these days; I don't like it when you scold me and when you're impatient with me, but I'd rather have that attention than nothing.

*Things would be different if you gave me attention when I'm good. I'm happy to play on my own, and talk to myself, and sing, but I need you to notice me **sometimes** when I'm good. Please, Mummy. Please, Dad. I miss you. **I'd love you to pay attention to me when I'm not misbehaving. I'll misbehave much less if you do.** I need the positive attention you used to give me – the affection, and the cuddling, and the delight when you looked at me. I need to know you love me and that I'm still loveable. Am I?...*

please notice me sometimes when I'm good

Giving positive attention

One of the goals of this book is to show the effects on children of giving them **positive, respectful attention, *even for a few minutes at a time*, when they are *not* demanding it.** That is the theme of almost all the chapters. It applies to the ways we listen to children, talk with them, touch them and play with them. Research shows that even the most 'difficult' children can respond to this approach; they find they no

longer need to misbehave because their parents are at last giving them the positive attention they had so desperately been seeking. Noticing children positively when they are *not* looking for attention helps to convince them that they are loveable and helps them grow in self-esteem and the ability to meet challenges *throughout* life.

What does it mean to 'pay positive attention?' Positive attention means communicating your love in the way you hold and carry and touch and stroke and cuddle your children, and in the way you talk with them, smile at them and listen to them. (According to one study, baby girls get five times as much cuddling and touch as boys!) Children pick up a great many messages about who they are and how welcome and loved they are, even in the first year of life. When you say things like "I'm glad you're a girl," "I'm glad you're a boy," or "I love you, and you are completely safe with me," the child may not know the meaning of the words but will still pick up the positive vibes from you – just as a baby picks up the negative vibes when described as 'spoilt' or 'demanding.'

In the first year of life, children's most basic task is to develop a sense of security and trust. This is done partly by meeting their needs, but also through all the positive communication and human closeness, the touching, the talking, the singing, that goes along with meeting their needs. When you take a few minutes to hold and comfort your crying daughter, you give her security and let her know she is loved.

Is it 'praise' or is it encouragement?

As children get older, one obvious way to give them positive attention is to notice any little contributions, efforts, or improvements they make. We can easily miss these because our society tends to emphasise success and achievement; people get prizes for coming first, not for making an effort or for improving. Try lowering your sights and forgetting about success or perfection. Even though your son cannot tie his laces, congratulate him on being able to make the *first* tying, "That's pretty good.

Well done." – or on making an unsuccessful attempt, "Good boy. That was really difficult, but you kept trying." Ignore the mess on the floor that has not been tidied and notice the *effort* your daughter makes to 'tidy' something – "Oh, I see you tidied away your *big* teddy. That helps me, thank you." Similarly, instead of noticing when your son leaves his coat on the floor (thus reinforcing the untidiness by giving attention to it), notice the one time when he hangs it up – and see how often he then begins to hang it up!

Note that parents do not go overboard with exaggerated or insincere praise in the situations above – "Oh, you're a wonderful boy! I don't know what I'd do without you!" Children know when you are being insincere and will often feel uncomfortable rather than encouraged by exaggeration. A child will often feel more encouraged by quite a low-key remark that just *notices* an effort or contribution. "Andrew's asleep because you sang to him. That's nice." "I was pleased to see you sharing your toys – was that hard?" Even a simple "thank-you" is often enough – "Oh, thanks for putting Teddy back."

'Praising' rather than encouraging a child also tends to make it harder for the child to live up to an adult's opinion – "You're a very generous girl" is much harder to live up to than "Mm, he was pleased you gave him that." Similarly, a remark like "That's a lovely drawing" gives *my* opinion and may not encourage children to form their own opinions, whereas an observation like "Mm, you've a lot of yellow in it – that makes it look brighter," or "You've worked hard at that," even "You've done that all by yourself," can help them to make up their own minds and develop their own creativity.

You notice in the statements above that **encouraging parents tend to speak personally, saying how they** *feel* – "I like..." "I was pleased to see..." "That helps me." "I'm happy about the way you've..." Can you see how "I like your picture" is better than a general statement like "That's a beautiful picture!" in helping a child develop a sense of it being okay for different people to have different tastes?

Do you give your child responsibilities? Now, we have seen that children need to experience limits, correction and some guidance for responsibility. Being a positive parent does not mean being a dear old Dreamy Dad or Doormat Mum who makes no demands. Children need to develop a sense of being able to do things well and make good decisions. Our goal as parents, then, is to help them grow gradually in responsibility so that they become responsible, caring, co-operative adults, able to contribute to society in their unique ways. How do we do this?

"Do not do for children what they can do for themselves," is what the psychologist Rudolf Dreikurs taught, for he had observed that children become more responsible when they are *given* responsibility. What effect will it have if you sort out squabbles, build lego houses, etc., instead of *helping* children to do these things for themselves? It will take more time initially, but you are developing your child's self-confidence and sense of responsibility when you take the time to ask questions and help her work out her own solutions: "I don't know... What do you think yourself?... How do you feel about that?..."

In the planning section at the end of this chapter, you will see many areas where

through all the positive communication

parents can let go and encourage their children to develop. This is usually done in three stages:

1. You do *most* of the work, helping your child to use a spoon, or to dress, or to ride a tricycle...

2. You do less and less, encouraging the child to do more each time by noticing the effort and improvement. Instead of picking up a ball and bringing it over, allow and encourage your baby to crawl over to get it. It is encouraging for children to learn by *doing* things that there are more and more things they are capable of.

3. You fade into the background – but you turn up occasionally to notice the improvement. "Look – she's feeding herself!" "Mm, you remembered to wash your hands. Well done!" If your encouragement is genuine, a child cannot ever get too much of it.

Time for guidance

Why is it that it is sometimes so difficult to get children to take on responsibilities? Sometimes, it may be because we push before they show readiness or interest. Each child is different, but if other children are potty-trained at his age, we may think he *ought* to be ready. We have to be patient! If Neil will go nowhere without his blanket or his Teddy, or if Anna still sucks her thumb at five, perhaps we need to respect their need for a security object until they are ready to let it go – that is part of their growth in security.

Or perhaps they are ready to take on responsibilities, but our *timing* is wrong. Probably the worst time for instruction or guidance is when we are under pressure or tired, or when a child has just made a mistake. Yet those are precisely the times when parents most *discourage* children by nagging, shouting, correcting or 'teaching.' We become critics then instead of guides.

That seems to point to **the importance of setting aside quieter, more relaxed times for helping a child to learn – and perhaps not even *attempting* guidance at other times.** Some parents link certain specific times with developing this

You remembered to wash them. Well done.

responsibility – like a weekly trip to a supermarket. That can slow you down and help you remember that the child is more important than the shopping. Somehow it seems not to matter then if the shopping takes an extra fifteen minutes – the shopping trip can become a thoroughly enjoyable outing as you point to the sugar, say "Get me the sugar, please" and wait for it to be delivered. Even if your son drops the sugar on the floor, it's no big deal – and both you and he go home in such good spirits that you may even enjoy giving him further responsibilities when it comes to stacking away the groceries.

An occasional encouraging remark will add to your child's experience: "Thanks for doing that." "I like you helping me." But it is the *experience* of helping you and of doing things for themselves that is probably better for building children's self-confidence than anything you *say*. Also the experience of your smile, your trust in her ability, your obvious enjoyment of his company, the occasional touch that says "I notice you and I like being with you" – these carry the more important messages in building your child's self-esteem.

When parents begin to allow children to take on new responsibilities, however, it sometimes happens that they overlook the effect of all this on a younger child. It is easy to keep the youngest child in a 'baby' role within a family so that even *less* is expected of her. Some psychologists suggest that it may be better not to continue to refer to that child as 'the baby,' but by name, and that you might give her some responsibilities at the same time as another child – like helping you 'wash' a door. In this way, she avoids the danger of becoming stuck in a role and she also has a positive, encouraging experience.

Encouragement is a way of life
Encouragement has to be genuine to be effective. One little boy, asked by his father to "come back and close the door, love," asked "Why do you only call me 'love' when you say not-nice things?" His father was shocked to realise that his irritation had been coming through in this way. Children are quick to pick up little clues – like the difference between *what* you say and *how* you say it. They are not fooled.

Genuine encouragement, then, is not just a matter of using *techniques* or trying to manipulate children to do what you want them to do. It is more a question of paying attention to the *child* than to his *behaviour*. **Learning techniques or skills may *help* you to become more encouraging, but encouragement is a mentality, a way of looking at children that respects them and wants them to develop in their own unique way.** It is a mentality that thinks about a child when she is not around, asking, "What is the next step that is going to stretch her and build her confidence, and how can I deal with my own irritations to be able to get enough distance to help her?" That can begin to colour your approach to *everyone* you meet.

But I'm just not a warm person!
This may seem like a tall order. What if you are just not a warm person? What if you do not even like *yourself* very much, or the kind of person you are? What if you are naturally a bit distant and critical – or if

Even if your son drops the sugar...

a child is driving you up the wall? It's usually a great relief to have a place where you can talk about how mad or guilty or bad you feel – perhaps in a parent support group. But it may help to know that being an encouraging person is also something you can grow into. It means slowing down, being more relaxed, making *time* for a child – and for your partner and others. You say 'no' to the unreasonable demands of your job, you let go of the fascination with keeping your home and children looking perfect, you resist the pressure to be always active and doing – or whatever else it is that absorbs your time.

That will take time and planning. As you learn to slow down and practise the skills in this book, however, the experience will gradually begin to affect you and you can *become* a warmer person. Then, this course ceases to be just about parenting and becomes something deeply fulfilling for yourself as a person. One of the great pieces of wisdom that has come from the East is that the secret of happiness is to be grateful, to be appreciative. Try it and see. The first step may be your decision to slow down and make the time to pay positive attention to your children when they are not expecting it.

Importance of *your* self-esteem

Doesn't this also point to the importance of encouraging *yourself*? You can be more positive in how you think about your children when you are positive in how you think about yourself. Try interrupting negative thoughts about yourself as soon as you become aware of them, and *remind* yourself that you're doing okay, and it is all right not to be perfect.

Similarly, **don't you need to be good to *yourself* if you want to be good to your child?** If you're not relaxed, your child will pick up the vibes. In chapter one we saw how important it is to get exercise, rest and fresh air. You need to *find* ways of getting these – even for your child's sake. It also helps to *speak* these values: if you say, "I went for a swim and I'm feeling great now," that may teach an important lesson.

Part of looking after yourself, too, is looking after your relationships – with a partner, with friends, or with your extended family. It is hard to go it alone. You need support. If you are a couple, everyone will suffer if your partner is squeezed out. When you make time for going out together, and for fun and teasing and laughter, you may both begin to feel better about yourselves. If possible, develop and encourage the bond, not just between mother and child but also between father (or a father figure) and child – and between you and your partner.

Summing up

This chapter is about the power parents have to encourage their children and help them grow in their ability to meet life's challenges. To sum up, **children develop and grow best, and they benefit in all kinds of ways, when their parents stop paying so much attention to misbehaviour and give them positive attention that they are not expecting.** This is not just a matter of encouraging *words*. It includes time for listening, singing, touching, cuddling, smiling, playing, laughing... The effect, even on a disruptive child, is magic. The idea is to stop looking for perfection and to concentrate on **little improvements or efforts instead of successes or achievements.**

This encouragement needs to be sincere, for children quickly sense when it is exaggerated or false. They also develop and grow in confidence when they are allowed to make decisions and are trusted with increasing responsibility instead of being sheltered or overprotected or expected to obey adults on demand.

Finally, there can be an important spin-off effect on *yourself* when you take a more encouraging approach. This is particularly true when you take time to relax and look after yourself, and when you interrupt and challenge negative thoughts about yourself.

In the remaining chapters of this book, you will find many other ways of encouraging children – even in the chapter on discipline (when you pick up and remove a kicking, screaming child from a supermarket, it may not *feel* like the most encouraging thing in the world, but it can be very positive and encouraging for that child to experience the security of firm limits!) In the next chapter, we will be looking at one of the most encouraging of all parenting skills – listening.

"I went for a swim and I'm feeling great now"

21

TABLE 2: ENCOURAGING CHILDREN'S DEVELOPMENT

Tick two ways in which you tend to discourage (columns 1 & 2), and two ways in which you tend to be reasonably good at encouraging (columns 3 & 4).

HOW PARENTS *DISCOURAGE*	TYPICAL BEHAVIOUR OR REMARKS	HOW PARENTS *ENCOURAGE*	TYPICAL BEHAVIOUR OR REMARKS
1. Tries to 'stretch' child too quickly.	Teaching to crawl, potty training, etc., too early. Or toys too advanced.	1. Respects child's own pace. Waits for readiness and interest.	Potty-training, walking, suitable toys, only when ready/ interested.
2. Exaggerated praise – based on *your* standards.	*What a beautiful painting – you're a wonderful boy!*	2. Happy with *efforts* rather than perfection.	(smiling) *You tried really hard. Good for you!*
3. Does too much for child.	*No, sit down – I'll put on your shoes.*	3. Allows child to experiment and make mistakes.	*You* put on the shoe and we'll buckle it together.
4. Forces child into new situations.	*Don't be silly – the dog won't bite you! Here! Pat his back.*	4. Doesn't push. Respects child's fears.	(lifting child) *Bye, doggie! See you tomorrow.*
5. Over-protective.	*Ah-ah!... Dirty! Don't touch the ground!*	5. Allows child to explore – and to play creatively.	*Would you like to splash the water and see?...*
6. Expects child to 'grow up' too quickly.	Removes favourite blanket/ teddy, or weans off bottle before ready.	6. Reasonably accepting and relaxed at each stage.	Weans off bottle or blanket when child shows interest in next stage.
7. Compares to others.	*Look how well **he** does it. When are you going to...?*	7. Happy with small improvements.	*Mm... You're much better at using the spoon now...*
8. Bosses, shouts, gives orders, controls.	*You're not trying! Eat it up fast and stop talking! Fast!*	8. Allows child to live with consequences – within reason.	*Not yet. You can have toast when you finish your cereal.*
9. Too busy to give child relaxed time/ attention.	*Would you stop whinging! I can't do everything!*	9. Spends time when child does *not* expect it – cuddles, listening, stories.	*What would you like to play?* Or: *I'm rushed now but we'll have special time at seven o'clock.*

CASE STUDIES

What might you do or say to encourage your child in some of the following situations? (Remember that it is also encouraging for children to experience some limits on their behaviour – though they may react and cry at the time.)

- Your baby has been frightened by a loud noise.
- You would like to help Delia learn to tidy up her toys after play.
- Jordan is learning to put on his shoes.

- You've been shopping, and two-year-old Katie wants to help you tidy away the groceries.
- Clare keeps opening cupboards in the kitchen and pulling everything out of them.
- You'd like to teach David to ride his tricycle.
- Duncan loves his bath and cries every time he's taken out of it.
- Julie refuses to eat mashed potatoes, but asks for "ice-queem."
- Richard puts his hands into his cereal and likes to play with it.

PLANNING

It is important not to 'push' children to learn to do things before they show some readiness or interest. Here are some things parents do for their children up to six or seven years old which their children, according to age, might learn to do for themselves. Put the first letter of your child's name beside anything which that child might now be ready to learn to do:

Crawl or walk instead of being carried.
Pick toys, etc., off floor.
Tidy away some groceries.
Wipe nose with tissue or cloth.
Take off some clothes.
Choose what to wear.
Put on some clothes.
Reach for some things.
Play with water.
Lay the table.
Ride a tricycle – or bike with stabilisers.

Ride a bicycle – without stabilisers.
Put soiled clothes in clothes basket.
Wash face and hands.
Paint, use crayons, draw.
Help with shopping in supermarket.
Settle own fights and squabbles.
Use a spoon, or knife, or fork.
Use scissors.
Hold own cup or bottle for drinking.
Eat with less supervision.
Put on shoes – and buckle/tie them.

*Choose one idea from the list above that you will introduce in the coming week. With which child are you going to try it? Making a **decision** to slow down and take time usually helps a parent to be more patient and positive, so when will **you** be able to relax and let go? What might be a positive approach? Remember to notice little improvements, or even efforts, "Thanks for doing that – it helps me." (And do remember to notice and encourage the **adults** in your life too!)*

My plans _____

_____

- ***Please read chapter three of your handbook before the next session.***

CHAPTER 3: LISTENING MEANS PAYING ATTENTION

"He was no problem. His tears dried up as soon as you left and he's been a happy, contented little boy ever since."

The teacher's words were music to Sarah Jeffrey's ears, for her son, Jack, had been screaming when she had left him at the play-school earlier.

"Hello, Jack," she said, "I believe you've been enjoying yourself!"

Ian ran over to his mother, let her lift him into her arms – and burst into tears!

"Mummy's bad," he said, between sobs.

"Mummy's bad!"

The teacher was taken aback. Later, she confided in a colleague, "I think the mother's the problem there. The child was perfectly happy until she appeared."

How wrong can you be! The mother was *not* the problem. **The real problem is that many people do not realise the importance of what is going on under the surface for children, and the important part played by children's** *feelings.* Jack may have appeared to play normally in his mother's absence, but inside he was full of pent-up feelings of insecurity and confusion and fear. *Now* he could sob because, in the security of his mother's arms, he felt free and safe enough to sob and release those feelings. His tears were a compliment to his mother. Because of her,

he will feel less fearful and confused the next time he is left at play-school.

When I come in from work, it's a constant demand for attention. Almost like something that can't be satisfied. So this week, I sat her up on the kitchen table, got down to her eye level and gave her full attention. After about two minutes, she was satisfied! She was happy to go off and play again.

Feelings are important

If Jack had not got this attention and security from his mother, what might have happened? Children who do not get good attention tend to misbehave. They misbehave when their feelings cannot be expressed or are not accepted and have to be repressed. Then, desperate for a chance to off load their distress, they demand your attention with all kinds of disruptive or aggressive behaviour – or in some cases by becoming extremely withdrawn and mistrustful of people and of life. Their behaviour is a coded cry for attention – "I am all mixed up and confused. It's almost as if I can't breathe – I need to scream or something."

Sometimes their feelings of distress are linked with something big – serious abuse or neglect, their parents' separation, the death of granny, or the death of a pet. But it's usually something much smaller – the common little hurts and bruises, physical or emotional, of every day, the misunderstandings, the discouraging remarks, the sense of failure in performing some task, being compared to someone else... These many little distresses, not expressed, can then build up to something enormous and disabling and even store up trouble for later life. But when parents recognise feelings and allow them to be expressed, children can learn that they can deal with their feelings without misbehaving.

What can parents do? Are there methods of listening that are especially good for allowing children to feel safe enough and secure enough to accept their feelings and express them freely? The purpose of this chapter is to offer some tips on listening to children in a respectful way so that this can happen. You can choose those ideas that might work best for you.

1. Pay attention
The first suggestion is that you pay attention. Try this – every now and then, put everything else aside and take a few minutes to *notice* your child. Really notice. You will need to look as well as listen, perhaps getting down on the floor or lifting her up to be at the same eye level – **eyes are more important than ears for listening.** Touch also helps. A child sitting cuddled in your lap will usually feel safer and find it easier to be herself.

Sitting cuddled in your lap

As you pay attention, see if you can think of a word that might sum up how the child *feels*. One parent claimed she gained a lot by switching off the one o'clock news to pay attention to her eight-month-old son, asking herself, "How is he right now?

What is he feeling?" The fact that her son could not talk did not bother her. There were all kinds of clues – the noises he made, his eyes, face, hands...

It is the same with toddlers and pre-schoolers – being able to talk does not mean they will tell you what they feel, but their 'body language,' including their tone of voice and the way they hold themselves, is full of clues.

2. Name the feeling
When you notice what the child is feeling, **try *naming* the feeling.** Here are some common feeling words that may help:

angry	annoyed	anxious
afraid	bored	comfortable
confident	delighted	disappointed
depressed	disgusted	embarrassed
excited	fed-up	furious
glad	great	happy
guilty	hopeless	hurt
left out	mad	miserable
over the moon	proud	relaxed
relieved	sad	satisfied
shy	silly	sore
stupid	thankful	upset
useless	willing	worried.

When you are learning this skill, one way to start is to say, "You feel... because..." For example, "You feel sad now because you miss Lata."

Later, when naming feelings becomes easier, you will find you can drop the 'because,' and speak more naturally, "You're sad Lata can't play with you today." "You're looking forward to your bottle, aren't you!" "You're excited that Harry is coming." "You seem to be a bit nervous about going to Amahl's party." "You're scared of Ginger..." or "Sounds like you're angry with me that I didn't allow you to stay..." (Your guess at the feeling will sometimes be wrong, but don't worry, a child will usually put you right.) You can name feelings at any time, even while disciplining children. If your daughter is enjoying colouring a picture and says, "No, I don't want dinner yet. I need to finish my picture," it will not help to scold or bark – "I said it was dinner-time!" You need to insist on her coming to dinner, but it is also respectful to *recognise* the feelings – and perhaps to offer a limited choice, "You love making the picture and you hate leaving it just now. That's hard for you... Do you want to go to dinner yourself, or do you want me to carry you?" She may still cry in frustration, but her feelings have been acknowledged and respected. If necessary, you can say, "It's okay to feel angry – I can understand that – and you can *say* you're angry, but I can't let you hit people or call them names."

The value of expressing feelings
"Okay," you may think, "Maybe feelings are important, but I'd feel stupid just saying, "You feel this" or "You feel that" – being like a mirror instead of a person! It's artificial! It's not me!"

If feelings were not important in your family as you grew up, this kind of mirror-listening, like any new skill, may indeed seem strange. But we already name things for our children all the time – cup, Teddy, milk, door. Why shouldn't we name feelings too? That gives a child permission to recognise feelings and become at ease with them instead of repressing them. It tells children that feelings are important – their own and other people's, and that ignoring them may be a lack of respect. Above all, **it brings feelings out into the open, so that they can be talked out instead of being acted out.**

Instead of making little of a child's fears, then, or saying, "Don't be silly. There's nothing to be afraid of," you might acknowledge the fear, "Yes, the flushing noise is scary, isn't it, but I need to flush the toilet to keep it clean."

In a parent support group recently, a father told how good it was to hear his son admit, "I'm jealous of Joanne because it's her birthday. I wish it was my birthday." He was happy because he realised how healthy it is for children to become *aware* of their feelings and be able to express them. Otherwise, they can be *controlled* by feelings, unaware of how they are being driven by them. Recent studies show that children (and adults) who express feelings

tend to think more clearly and make better decisions.

A chance to yell and bawl and cry
Unfortunately, one of the ways in which many children, especially boys, are cut off from their feelings is through not being allowed to cry. Parents want their children to 'feel better' and they mean well when they say, "Don't cry," or "Shsh" or "Don't upset yourself." But crying does not upset the child. **Crying *releases* the upset feelings. Tears are healing. When we cry, we release pain and hurt – like lancing a boil and letting the poison out.** How often people say after a good cry: "I feel better. That did me good." Children know this naturally. When little hurts and frustrations build up inside them throughout a day, they know they need a good cry and they begin to look for opportunities to yell and bawl and cry and let out all those nasty feelings of insecurity, doubt, anger, frustration, pain... But they need to feel safe to do that. They need parents who are not afraid of tears. They need parents who will *allow* them to cry.

Your daughter will not come and tell you, "I feel terrible – can I cry now?" She is more likely to make a nuisance of herself.

"You feel sad because you miss Lata"

She becomes demanding, but does not seem to know what she wants. She disagrees with anything you suggest, or picks fights with everyone in the family. You pick her up on your knee and try to get through to her, but even though you are holding her loosely she squirms and protests, "You're holding me too tight!" There is no need to argue with her – just continue to hold her loosely but firmly, and the tears may begin to come. At first, she will blame something unimportant for her upset – or she blames you and says she hates you. Let her be unreasonable if that helps her to cry and shout and release her pent-up feelings. Gradually, the real pain will come out. **It may take a few extra minutes now but may save you hours of difficult behaviour later.**

How to help children to cry!

When we are sensitive to what is going on, we *can* make it safer and easier for a child to cry and express feelings, encouraging her to thump a pillow or roar like a lion, stamp her feet or even draw her feelings with crayons. We can also encourage *tears*, knowing how helpful and healing they are. One of the best ways to do this seems to be to *stay* **with a crying baby or child, giving her good attention.** What does 'good attention' mean?

One good way to give attention is through touch. How often have you seen a toddler whimpering until he feels the safety of a hug – then bellowing and sobbing out his pain, safe in a parent's arms. Touch will only help sometimes, however. Saying understanding, loving things will often help – it may be such a contradiction to how your son feels inside to hear you say, "I love you" that he will explode into tears. You may not even know what the crying is about. That is not important – it is not the time to ask questions. Just hold your son close, but try to look gently and tenderly at the little pained face, if you can – your eyes will often communicate understanding and allow his tears to flow. **There is no need to speak while the tears are coming – words can interrupt crying.** Then,

instead of asking questions every time the sobbing dies down a little, try saying something else loving or understanding, "That's awful for you," or "You're feeling terrible," or "You felt that was very unfair." Notice that the crying will then often get louder – it may even become screaming as he feels permission to off load some more of those bottled-up feelings. That is perfectly normal once a child is given good attention and 'permission' to release the pain. The crying may last as much as five minutes – or longer. Don't worry – the tears are healing. Look at him as he calms down. Notice how clear his eyes have become. See how he has been healed...

Parents who give this kind of attention to a crying child, even once, can become so convinced of the healing power of tears that they change their entire attitude to crying and become more available to a child. You may like to try an experiment – the next time your child is upset about something, try taking her up in your arms and 'helping' her to cry, and notice the effects afterwards. But *do* notice the effects – if a child is *constantly* crying, and you've given good attention and don't see an improvement, it is possible that she is seeking attention on demand with her tears.

tears are healing

Play-listening

Right through this book, we have seen how encouraging it is to children to notice them when they are not expecting your attention, and to tell them what you have noticed. That is why naming the feelings we notice is such a helpful way of 'listening' to a child. The child *feels* noticed and accepted just as she is.

Another powerful way of listening and noticing (and one that feels just as strange and unnatural at the beginning!) is 'play-listening.' **With 'play-listening' you give your child good attention and a sense of being 'noticed,' partly by silently watching her play, and partly by saying what you see her doing.** (It is best not to *ask* what she is doing – when children are doing something they enjoy, a question can easily distract them and *interrupt* their play). You quietly join her, even for a few minutes, kneeling beside the table she is playing at, or lying on the floor beside her. You mirror, not just the *feelings* you notice, but *anything* you notice about her as she plays. Notice what she is doing, and say (between pauses of perhaps half a minute) what you see, "You're painting a picture... Lots of green in it... You're wondering what colour to use next..." Or similarly, "Oh, you're playing with the lego... That's three bricks together now… Ah, you found the place..."

It does not help to go into ecstasies about how pretty her picture looks, or how brilliant the lego construction is. 'Play-listening' is low-key, quiet and respectful. You may be tempted to say "What a beautiful picture!" That is okay, but **a noticing comment is more respectful in helping her to be creative, to assess and judge her own work, and not be over-influenced by your opinions – and it does not interrupt her train of thought.** With 'play-listening,' you observe in silence most of the time. At times, you may like to name your *own* positive feelings, "I *like* your castle" or "I like watching you," but most of what you say will be simple 'noticing' comments. You know how *you* feel when things you say or do go unnoticed, so saying such obvious, ordinary things is not silly or unnecessary. Your child feels 'noticed,' important to you, encouraged and valued. Her self-esteem

grows, her natural desire to be good blossoms, and misbehaviour tends to lessen.

I lay down on my tummy beside Eileen and just watched her. "You're playing with the baskets," I said. "Yes," she said, engrossed. "You're putting things into them," I said. "This one hasn't got enough in it," she replied. I was tempted to ask why, or to say how well she was doing – typical patronising comment – or to suggest what to do next. I didn't. I stayed silent, just commenting now and then on what I saw. I don't think she looked at me once – but she knew I was there and I knew she felt good about that. I enjoyed the experience. And it's so simple anyone can do it.

The effects of 'play-listening'
Take the case of five-year-old Arun. He was as disruptive a child as you could imagine. He was banned from play-school because he kept turning over boxes of toys and containers of paint on the floor, but chiefly because of the damage he had done to other children by head-butting and biting. At home he drove his parents to breaking point and was almost totally out of control in spite of their best efforts. In desperation they turned to social services and the whole family was referred to a clinic that specialised in working with disruptive children and their families.

Progress was slow at first, but gradually Arun softened and became a normal, reasonably co-operative child as a result of experiencing *firm limits* and *positive attention* from his parents. The limits were essential so that less attention would be given to his misbehaviours, but it was the positive attention to his play that caused the breakthrough. **Once the parents learned to 'play-listen' instead of ignoring Arun at play, the effect was dramatic.**

But you will not normally notice anything dramatic during a session of 'play-listening.' You may wonder what all the fuss is about. You may feel frustrated –

most parents find it difficult to hold themselves back from asking questions or making suggestions or getting involved in 'helping' the child to play. One mother was even told, "I don't want you here when I'm playing," (and she wisely decided to respect that). If you persevere, however, it is over a period that you will see the benefits, whether with a baby, a toddler, or an older child. You will learn a great deal about parenting, about listening and respecting and not pushing your own ideas or interfering with children. And you will learn to enjoy them more.

Other ways of giving attention

There are other, more obvious ways of listening and giving good attention to children. If you want more communication with your son, it is worth asking yourself *when* is he in a mood for talking – **you can sometimes have great chats lying in bed beside a child in the darkness after settling him.**

You may also like to think about what *kind* of questions help – "What did you do at play school today?" is usually a conversation stopper. Try a more *specific* question – "Which of the boys were you playing with?" or "Where do you think we should go on Sunday?" or "What's your best memory of...?" or "Show me what you painted today... Mm, a lot of bright colours... Who's this in the middle?"

Questions, we have seen, may interrupt a child's play, but at other times, they may be the springboards you need to get her to talk. They are better than solutions when your child comes to you with a problem. "What do you think you could do about it?" shows respect for her judgement instead of giving your own opinion. Similarly, when she shows you a drawing, you might ask what *she* thinks of it first before saying what *you* like about it. **Encouraging your child to talk is a great investment in your future relationship with her.**

As your child talks, all the skills we have already mentioned will apply – looking, touching, naming feelings, silence... Sometimes, it helps to repeat a few words he has just said to encourage him to keep talking and let him know how interested you are. "I see... So you want to be a dad when you're big..." An occasional nod or grunt will often help, or a single word that allows him to continue without feeling interrupted – "Mm..." "Yes..." "I see..." "Oh..." But doing this must not become a 'technique.' **Your goal is to communicate respect, and a child will know if you are just going through the motions!**

Showing interest in a child's story and encouraging her to talk also applies to a baby who has no words. You can 'listen' to the wonderful things she is communicating to you, glad to have your full attention.

listening to a baby who has no words

Go easy on yourself

But you are not Superparent. Giving this kind of attention to children is something you can practise and improve *some* of the time, but it should not become a new set of rules or obligations to make you feel guilty. There will be times when it is perfectly okay to *show* a child how to use a toy or make a sand castle with a plastic bucket. Your new listening skills are not to be used all the time – your children would become pretty bored if you spent your time naming what you saw them feeling or doing! Life has to go on, too, with all its pressures. Try to plan a few times for special listening in the week, but there will often be times when you are too busy or too stressed or too tired to listen. It will help if you explain, "I'd love to hear about it, but I can't listen right now. Will you tell me about it after dinner?"

Sometimes you will not show respect. You will shout and scold and listen to nobody. You may even know in your heart you are doing all the 'wrong' things. But that is life. You're human. Nobody is perfect. And **the goal is not to *be* perfect. Be gentle with yourself: ask forgiveness of your child later, then forgive your*self*, and move on.**

For the past week my wife and I have tried that suggestion of a few minutes' listening time each way. It sounds a bit artificial, but we find it's nice to have a few minutes of uninterrupted listening time – instead of the usual, "You think you've had a bad day – wait till you hear about mine!"

That brings us to the topic of caring about ourselves. If children are often driven by blocked feelings that prevent them from acting freely or thinking clearly, so are adults. We can convince ourselves we are acting logically, but that is often because we are out of touch with our feelings – feelings like guilt about how we are bringing up our children, fear of what people will think if the house is not tidy, or hurt with a partner or family member. **When you take a minute or so to *notice* what is driving you, those feelings begin to have less control over you. Better still if you can share what you feel with a partner or friend.** What better way to look after your close relationships than to take a few minutes regularly to give the same kind of respectful attention and listening to each other! A number of marriage courses recommend that couples make a date to set aside 15-20 minutes twice a week just to share their feelings about their lives, their work, their stresses, their plans.

Summing up

In previous chapters we have seen the importance of giving children positive attention when they are not expecting it. Listening is a powerful way to do that, so we have looked, in this chapter, at different ways of listening more positively and actively to children – **not just listening with our ears, but with our eyes and arms and body position, and with what we say.** This kind of listening is more an attitude and a mentality, however, than a set of techniques or skills, so we need to feel okay in ourselves in order to tune in. The key to this attitude is to pay attention to the child.

This has many spin-offs. **Children who are shown respect and concern learn to respect themselves and become more confident** (just as children who are ignored develop low self-esteem and believe that they *deserve* to be ignored). They also become aware of their feelings and can express them more freely instead of acting them out. This helps them learn to respect others and to listen and show concern in turn.

When we make the decision to listen well, even for five minutes at a time, we can do wonderful things for a child.

a few minutes' listening time each way

TABLE 3: WAYS OF LISTENING

*Here are eight tips on improving our listening to children. Listening well is difficult, so these tips should not be allowed to depress you. Which **one** or **two** ways of improving your listening most appeal to you?*

---

1. PAYING ATTENTION Children can sense when your attention is genuine. Stop what you are doing occasionally and take time out to *notice* your child and to pay attention to what she is doing or saying – especially when she is not demanding attention. If children only get attention when misbehaving, you can expect more misbehaviour!

---

2. EYE-LISTENING Your eyes are usually more important than your ears for listening. It helps to get down to the same eye-level and see what your child is feeling. How do *you* feel when someone listens to you without looking at you?

---

3. TOUCH-LISTENING A parent touching, cuddling, or hugging him will often help a young child to express feelings more fully, including fears, affection, anger, tears, and lots of other feelings he can't put into words.

---

4. PLAY-LISTENING A child thrives on good attention – not just when she is upset. Play-listening means giving her good attention and a sense of being 'noticed,' partly by silently watching her play, and partly by saying what you see her doing: *"Mm, you've put the doll sitting up there."*/ *"Ah, you found the right place..."*/ *"Mm, you've used three of them now..."*

---

5. SILENCE You may have to bite your tongue in order not to argue or reason with an upset child. An upset child usually doesn't want to hear explanations, however reasonable – he may just want to be unreasonable, to scream and rage and say how unfair everything is! Only when he gets all that off his chest will he be open to listening to you.

---

6. SINGLE WORDS Sometimes, one or two words may be enough to give your child a sense that you are listening and that you understand. *"Mm..." "Oh..." "Really?..." "I see..." "Oh, no!..."* But a child will know if you are just going through the motions and not really listening.

---

7. REPEATING Repeating a few of your child's words, or summing up what she said, perhaps after a pause, can also let her know that you are paying attention and you understand. *"Oh, dear! Your lovely tricycle!..."*/ *"So that's what you're going to do today..."* That may encourage her to say more.

---

8. REFLECTING FEELINGS Noticing what your child is feeling and checking that out with him, can help him to become aware of his feelings, trust you, and become freer in himself: *"So you're **sad** it's broken..."*/ *"You're **angry** I won't let you do that..."*/ *"You sound **pleased** that granny's coming..."*

GETTING IN TOUCH

1. What are some feelings a child might have when (s)he...

...asks, "Why do doggies bark?"

...says, "I hate you!"

...soils pants, or wets the bed, although (s)he's been toilet trained.

...keeps crying, but doesn't want a bottle.

...smiles and gurgles to self.

2. What are some negative ways in which parents react to the situations above instead of listening, e.g., when they are busy or in a bad mood?

CASE STUDIES

1. Questions, corrections, instructions, warnings, etc., are necessary at times, even though they are not 'noticing' comments. Can you pick out any of the comments below that you think are examples of **'noticing'** what the child is doing? (i.e., 'play-listening') – though much obviously depends on the speaker's tone of voice!

a). What are you going to do with the ball?

b). You're going off with your ball to play.

c). No, don't go over there with the ball!

d). Why did you take the ball there?

e). That was a good hard kick!

f). Give me the ball, and I'll show you how to kick it.

g). You're getting better at kicking it!

h). Careful with the ball! Stay away from the baby!

2. Can you think of some 'noticing' comments you could make to a child in the situations below? (You might 'notice' colours, garments, shapes, actions, etc.) The child is...

a) playing in sand. b) dressing dolls and putting them to bed. c) building a lego house.

PLANNING

1. You are not expected to listen attentively all the time, but how will you make at least one child special by setting aside some time for 'listening,' perhaps two or three times in the coming week? Which child will you listen to? When and where will that child tend to be more receptive? – bedtime? bath time? at play?... What might help? – Eye-listening? 'Noticing' comments? Silence? Cuddling or touching?... (Note that listening is just as important for babies/ infants as it is for other children – they thrive on 'play-listening,' 'touch-listening' or 'eye-listening' long before they can talk.)

2. Would you like to arrange with your partner to have a regular time in the evening, or a few times a week, for listening to each other? You might talk, for example, about what's been happening for you recently, what you've been thinking, and how you've been feeling. (If you do not have a partner, you may like to make a similar arrangement with a friend – many people find it easier to cope with tensions and stresses when they can talk them out with someone.)

My plans _____

_____

• *Please read chapter four of your handbook before the next session.*

CHAPTER 4: TALKING WITH YOUR CHILD

"You're becoming a bully!"

There was a thud on the floor above, followed by a child's scream.

"What is going on!" Frank roared, as he tore up the stairs, "What has got into you both this morning! You haven't given me *one* minute's peace!" Upstairs, he continued to shout at the children, "Jordan, what do you think you're doing? You're becoming a little *bully*! And you wipe that smirk off your face, Janice, because you're just as bad – you haven't stopped pestering me all morning... Do you think I have nothing better to do than run up and down these stairs!..

Even as he shouted, Frank knew in his heart that he was making the situation worse. What he was doing was pointless, ineffective, negative, even abusive. He himself was doing the real bullying. Yet he felt as if he had little control over how he was acting.

And it was understandable. Frank was exploding with feelings that needed an outlet. He had been made redundant at work three months ago, and he resented being stuck at home minding children. This morning, he felt particularly helpless and worried for he had just heard that his mother, who lived far away, had broken her hip. The children's normal fighting and squabbling had irritated him a lot recently, but it was driving him crazy today.

"It sounds worse when I'm upset"

Back downstairs, he sat down and sank his head in his hands. Time to think. And to feel. "I'm not coping well. I don't want to be like this. What am I going to do?..."

A few moments later, it was clear to him: "I know. I'll *tell* them."

He went upstairs again and sat on the bed in the children's room.

"I need to talk with you for a minute." His voice already sounded softer. His feelings were no longer controlling him. *He* was taking control.

Five-year-old Jordan and three-year-old Janice looked up, uncertain.

"Listen, I'm in terrible form this morning. I've just got news about granny. She fell and broke her hip – that's this part here – and she's in hospital. I'm sure the doctors and nurses are looking after her well, but I wish we could see her. I'm sorry for shouting and saying those things. I didn't mean them – I was just upset. I love you both, but your squabbling sounds worse when I'm upset. Can you understand that?"

What happened next surprised Frank. Jordan came over and put his arms around him. Janice followed. Deciding to tell his children how he was feeling had changed a nasty situation into a moment of closeness.

a moment of closeness

A *you-message* or an *I-message*?

Think about what happened there. You notice that the first time Frank spoke with the children, his voice was raised, he was name-calling, faultfinding, attacking, not respectful. It was all 'you, you, you.' There are eight different 'you-messages' in what he said. **When someone uses the word 'you' a lot in an aggressive tone of voice, we can be pretty sure they are in a negative, blaming mood, putting people down and discouraging them.**

The second time Frank spoke with the children, the big difference was that he used 'I' messages. He spoke personally instead of blaming. He used 'I' instead of 'you.' He took responsibility for his own feelings and said how he felt (I'm in terrible form, I'd love.., I'm sorry.., I was upset..)

This is not always easy to do. You may need to cool down first before you can talk. Or maybe you need to talk with a friend to off load some of your stronger feelings. But when you can speak personally, it is generally more effective. Even if it had not been effective, however, even if it had made *no* difference, it was *respectful*.

How we fail to show respect
That is what we are looking at in this chapter – how we can talk more respectfully with children. Perhaps a good starting point is to become more aware of the ways in which we *fail* to respect them. Very often, like Frank above, we would not dream of harming or frightening a child, but we can easily end up doing just that, without thinking; when we are weary, annoyed, or impatient and we react with anger or rage, unaware that **small children cannot understand or cope with raw adult emotions.** Or we dismiss children with "I don't want to hear any tales" – with the result that they may trust us less and we do not hear things we need to hear. Or we make scary threats like, "If you do that again, I'll give your Teddy away to one of those good boys!" or, "I'm going to get the police" (some of us even make God into a kind of policeman – "And remember – when I'm not here, God can still see you!") In doing this, we usually have no idea of the harm we may be doing or the long-term effect on the child. Some of our 'you-messages' may include words like thoughtless, stupid, rude, clumsy, bad, stubborn, lazy, mean, selfish, liar, idiot, pest, bully, thief, and so on. These names can stick, and may influence a child's thinking, sometimes for life.

But perhaps the main way we do not show respect is with the constant barrage of instructions and corrections delivered to a child in a bossy voice. Can you imagine how your visitors would feel if you talked to them as you talk to your child? – *"What did I tell you to do with that coat? Hang it up!... Not there – on the hook!... Are you blind? – there! Now, get onto the chair and eat up! Without a word!... Not there – that's my chair, and you know it! Come on, hurry up! You don't have to take all day! Eat up, I said. Now, look at the mess you've made! – a little pig would have more manners! Here, wipe your face!... That's not wiped – wipe it properly!... Come on, no talking, just finish!... Now, out you go to the garden and talk to Andrew! No fighting!... And don't let me see any mud on those trousers when you come back!..."*

How many of your friends would want to come back? The relationship with your child will naturally suffer and the friendship between you will lessen. What can you do instead?

Using *I-messages*
One thing that helps is to **correct the *behaviour* but not the *person*.** It is better to say, "That was a naughty *thing* to do" than to say "You're a naughty little *girl*!" or "You're a lazy little *boy*!" or "You're stupid!" (It's best to say *exactly* what you didn't like, and not to use labels like 'naughty' or 'stupid' at all). Most 'you-messages' are unhelpful because they

"I'll give your Teddy away..."

34

blame or attack the *person* rather than the behaviour.

This is another advantage in using 'I' messages, for they, too, focus on behaviour rather than on the child – "I'm angry that you hit the baby – I won't take that behaviour."/ "When you shout like that, I get nervous you'll waken granny."/ "I'm annoyed you've spilt that when I've just cleaned the floor."

There is no guarantee that an 'I' message will *correct* a behaviour, but at least it does not attack the child and can be *part* of effective discipline (which we will look at in the next chapter).

Let's look at 'I' messages in more detail, for they offer a *respectful* way of talking with children. You use the word 'I' or 'me,' and:

☐ you simply say what you *feel* (*I'm annoyed* you got out of bed./ *I was glad* to see you playing with her./ *I don't like it* when you do that.)

☐ or you say what you *need* (I need you to be quiet./ I need a rest),

☐ or you say what your *position* is (I want you to eat with the spoon./ I can't allow you to do that).

Can you see how these statements do not accuse or attack? "I would like you to play quietly" is so much more respectful than "Hey! – don't be making so much noise in here!" – provided your tone of voice is also calm and firm.

Talked out or *acted* out

Sometimes parent educators can give the impression that everything will be okay if we only give the right 'I' messages to our children. 'I' messages, however, can be used too often. "Please pick that up off the floor" is not an 'I' message, yet it is a respectful request. The point is that a disapproving, impatient or critical *tone of voice* will obviously affect the way a child *experiences* what you say. Showing respect has more to do with *how* we speak than with *what* we say.

That said, what we are teaching children with a good 'I' message is that it is okay to have feelings and needs, and that

there are healthy ways of dealing with anger – **that anger can be *talked* out instead of being *acted* out.** (You might at least say you are too angry to talk it out until you calm down a bit.) But if you *shout* an 'I' message, if your tone of voice is aggressive or threatening, or if it sounds as if you are blaming the child for your feelings, then that is no longer an 'I' message.

Talking *positively*

'I' messages are not just for giving corrections. It is important to share your vulnerable feelings, your concerns for your children, and your positive feelings – what you enjoy, your hopes, your love. In chapter two, we saw how encouraging it can be for a child when you speak positively, using 'I' or 'me' – "That helped me – thank you."/ "I love you just the way you are."/ "I was happy when I saw you doing that."/ "One of the best things I ever did was to have you."/ "I was pleased you stopped when I asked you to – thank you."/ "Mm. I like your picture. Can I put it up on the wall?"/ "I like going for a walk with you."

Even 'I' messages that correct can be made more encouraging if you add a positive ending. "I don't like it when you're bossy because it hides the lovely gentle side there is to you."/ "I don't want you doing that to the baby because it hurts her – though I know you don't mean to hurt her."/ "I'm disappointed you left your toys like this, because you tidied them well yesterday – you did a good job."

This emphasis on being positive and respectful is the single most important point in this chapter. Right through the book, we have continually seen the importance of giving positive attention to children. It would be difficult to exaggerate its effect on a child's confidence, self-esteem and behaviour. But speaking positively does not come easily to many of us. Psychologists observing parents communicating with small children recorded the number of corrections, accusations, instructions, threats, yes/no questions, warnings and put downs they heard – and the number of friendly comments. They found very few friendly comments! Their conclusion was that, **even when parents are not speaking disrespectfully to their children, there is still a serious lack of *positive* communication in what is being spoken.** Corrections and instructions are a necessary part of parenting, but if positive communication is so essential for children's growth and development, isn't it sad when *most* of what we say is *Don't... Stop! No! Wait! Where did you leave your shoe? Hurry up! Why did you hit him? Be quiet! Eat up. Watch where you're going! Close the door. What are you crying about!*

So what can we do to make the way we talk with children a more positive, friendly experience for them?

"What would you like us to talk about?"

Talking with babies

Take babies first. A baby may not understand words, but she is remarkably sensitive and open to positive communication from a parent. She watches you carefully and senses your moods from the look on your face, the ways you touch her, your silence, your smile, your tone of voice... She does not need to understand your words to know that what you are saying is friendly and positive and warm. Parents seem to know that instinctively. Many of us are excellent at listening to and talking with babies and small infants. It does not worry us that infants cannot understand our words – we tend to smile and chat and say lovely, encouraging things.

It is good that we tell them often that we love them, for researchers have found in many studies that these **messages of love from a parent have a calming, reassuring effect, even on tiny infants.** In talking like this, we do far more than help a child's language development; we give him a great, positive start in life and we give him a sense of belonging and security.

Making *time* for talking

As children get older, they have the same need for positive attention. **They need to hear often that we love them, not just to guess it.** And they need us to continue to chat with them, tell them stories and 'notice' them positively. There are lots of opportunities for little snatches of conversation during the day. What about your talk at the table? – or while you work, travel, walk in the park, or visit the post office or shops? When you decide to cut back on corrections and warnings – or 'baby-talk!' – and to start a chat, you can help to build on children's experience, naming what you are seeing and doing, asking questions, stretching their language and horizons and their ability to think. (As you perform a task, you can also avoid sexism by making your daughter familiar with a screwdriver, a spade, a rake, and by making your son familiar with a sieve, a tin opener, sewing materials...) You will probably find that discipline and correction are less necessary once your child is engaged and interested.

Some parents tend to be pretty good at giving positive attention at bedtime, but it is best not just always to read stories from a book. Try stopping in the middle of a story and asking, "What do you think is coming next?" or "How do you feel about that?" In this way you encourage a two-way chat.

Children also love stories 'from your head,' especially stories about when you (or they) were small. Telling them stories about what they used to do when they were smaller helps to build their sense of belonging and self-worth. Stories about when *you* were small are equally helpful – you may find memories come flooding back as you talk about your childhood, about your first day in school, 'adventures' you had, how you got on with your friends, what your parents were like with you, what toys you had and how you played. **Children are fascinated with these stories, especially by what you were like when you were the age they are now. And this gives them a sense of their own roots.** It helps, of course, to look at a child as you are speaking, because eye contact will help communication (but don't insist on the child making eye contact with you). It also helps to be close, to be touching or cuddling a young child, perhaps to get into bed beside your pre-schooler and ask something like, "What would you like us to talk about?"

Where will they get their values?
As well as the obvious benefits arising from these chats, there is the added advantage of helping children to form values and develop their sense of right and wrong. After all, who is influencing your children or helping them decide what is important in life? Will they get most of their values from television, or from friends, or from you? **Studies show that you have far more influence on them than anyone else.** You do not need to have a degree or be a wonderful communicator: all you need is to be yourself and to spend time with them. When you tell stories, when you explain what is important to you and why you act as you do (as Frank did in the story at the beginning of this chapter), you reassure a child, you stretch her imagination and her world, you encourage her to think, and you influence her value system as it forms. You release a child from guilt, and change how he sees things, for example, when you

say something like, "As you know, Dad and I don't get on well, but it's not your fault – we're just very different and we've often disagreed about things, even before you were born."

A message for yourself
Finally, a word about how all this applies to your relationships with other adults. Do *you* talk to someone when you are upset? Do you talk out feelings like anger with another adult, or do you remain silent? – or do you act out your feelings by shouting, banging doors, or going off in a huff? 'I' messages are not just for talking with *children*. They help to communicate feelings and needs to *anyone*, especially to a partner, if you have one. "I need to talk with you about something. When can you listen?"/ "I'll clear the kitchen if you vacuum."/ "I'm happy to get up with the baby tonight if you get up tomorrow night."/ "I'd love a hug." **Open communication is a powerful way to build a relationship.** Speaking openly about your feelings and needs also gives a message and a model to children that it's okay for *them* to be in touch with feelings and to say what *they* feel and need. Your behaviour with a partner or with others close to you can teach children a great deal.

But keep in mind that the ideas in this book are only suggestions and guidelines, not new rules or 'shoulds.' Most of us will continue to fly off the handle at times – we will act on our feelings and forget to speak personally and respectfully, or we will say things in a hurtful, aggressive or impatient way. Then the most important 'I' message may be to come back soon with "I'm sorry. Please forgive me. I'm stressed at the moment and I wasn't thinking clearly."

Summing up
In this chapter, we have been looking at how we talk with children. We see that there is often a lack of respect in what we say and (especially) in our tone of voice. This is not deliberate. There may be deep feelings within us that make it difficult for us to speak calmly. A first step may be to

find someone to talk with – or a parent support group where we can talk frankly about our frustrations.

We won't change overnight, but it helps to use the word 'I' or 'me' instead of 'you.' It also helps to practise speaking more gently and respectfully, taking greater care to avoid an aggressive tone of voice. **When children live with intolerance, they learn to *be* intolerant; when they live with respect, they learn to respect themselves and others.**

A great deal of what we say to children from a year upwards consists of instructions, corrections, warnings and yes/no questions. There is a lack of balance when these account for *most* of what our children hear from us. We have seen throughout this book that a child thrives on positive, focused attention. When you are able to give this attention, you will have less *need* to give corrections, warnings or instructions, and you and your child will tend to get on much better together.

I'd love a hug

TABLE 4: TALKING WITH YOUR CHILD

Try ticking one of your weak points (column 1) and one of your strong points (column 2). Then mark two things in the second column you would like to improve at.

UNHELPFUL WAYS OF TALKING **Ways of talking that do not show respect to children.**	HELPFUL WAYS OF TALKING **Speaking respectfully and personally (using 'I' or 'me').**
1. THREATS It is scary for a child to hear thoughtless threats about ghosts or the police, or "the big dog outside," (or God!), or leaving her somewhere, or giving away his ball to a 'good' boy.	1. If you're upset, give an 'I' message. *I don't like it when you do things like that,* or: *I feel sad when you talk like that,* or, *I need time to think about this.*
2. NAME CALLING An occasional slip can't do much harm, but try not to call a child stupid, bad, lazy, rude, liar, idiot, thief... Names sometimes stick – for life.	2. But do say how you **feel** about the **behaviour** – *I'm annoyed you banged the door* (rather than a 'you' message like *You're rude!*)
3. BLAMING AND SHAMING In chapter two we saw that fault-finding and criticising often *increase* misbehaviour – and may do lasting damage.	3. Encouragement is like sunshine for a child, especially when it's personal: *I like you just the way you are. I love watching you play. I feel better after that cuddle.*
4. NO TIME FOR CHATS TV and toys may be educational and stimulating, but there is no substitute for some positive personal attention from **you**.	4. *As soon as your TV programme ends, we'll switch it off and have a chat. Will we talk about when **I** was small or when **you** were small?...*
5. SHOUTING IN ANGER If you act out anger and annoyance – slapping, shouting, or speaking in an aggressive tone – don't be surprised if your children end up doing the same.	5. Show you can **talk** out anger instead of **acting** it out – but watch your tone of voice: *When you do that to the baby, I feel so angry that I want to thump something.*
6. BABY TALK Some baby talk may be okay, but using it a lot may prevent a child's language from developing at its natural pace.	6. Natural talking stimulates a child's thinking and language. Using correct words (including for parts of the body), lays a good foundation for the future.
7. GIVING ORDERS Bossing and giving orders may get children to do what you want *now*, but they may resent you as a result – and it may not help them to form values.	7. It helps to explain *why* – to give your reasons or values: *If your tricycle gets rusty, I can't afford another./ I'm sorry I was so cross with you – I was very tired.*

GETTING IN TOUCH

*We need to give corrections/ instructions to our children, but it is a pity if **most** of what we say is correcting, instructing, etc. See if you agree with the way the first six sentences below are marked; then see if you can mark numbers 7-12, using one **each** of the letters opposite:*

C (for Correction),
A (for Accusation),
I (for Instruction),
P (for Put-down),
T (for Threat),
O (Open statement that is none of these)

1. "Leave the baby alone. Don't do that to her!" C
2. "I know why Andrew's crying – because you hit him!" A
3. "Put that down. It's dirty." I
4. "Are you stupid? How often do you have to be told!" P
5. "Do it fast – or you'll be sorry!" T
6. "It's going to rain today. There's a strong wind blowing." O

7. "Stop it. That's dangerous! "
8. "Would you shut up! – you never stop moaning!"
9. "If you don't get back into bed, you'll get a smack!"
10. "I wonder if Gran will arrive in time for dinner?"
11. "Now, close the door behind you, and pick up your Teddy."
12. "That's a lie!"

CASE STUDIES

*1. What are some **unhelpful** ways to correct a child in the situations below?*
- **Your son puts his head down and won't look at people you meet.**
- **Your daughter doesn't come when called for dinner.**
- **Toys are left scattered all over the floor.**
- **You're preparing dinner and the children's noise is too loud for you.**
- **Your toddler is whinging all day but won't play with anything.**

2. How could you speak respectfully to your child in each of the situations above? If you can think of an 'I' message, saying what you feel or need, all the better. (For example, in the first two situations you might say, a) "When you put your head down like that and don't look at people, I feel disappointed because people won't know how friendly you are." and b) (calmly – at least not aggressively) "I've spent a lot of time preparing dinner, and it makes me mad when you don't come."

PLANNING

Would you like to choose one of the following ways to talk more positively and respectfully with your child(ren) this week?

1. What is your worst time of the day for scolding/ speaking aggressively? What might help? – Get up earlier?... Think ahead?...
2. Babies may not understand *words*, but they certainly 'understand' your tone of voice and your undivided attention. When will you set a few minutes aside this week to talk to a baby or other child, giving positive, focused attention? What will you talk about?

3. How will you speak more *personally* over the next week – not just to your children but to a mother, partner, friend, workmate... Include *encouraging* 'I' messages as well.

My plans _____

_____

- *Please read chapter five of your handbook before the next session.*

CHAPTER 5: DISCIPLINE

"You can clear up your toys now, Nicholas. It will soon be story-time."

What Annette was asking was not unreasonable, for she had taken time to teach three-year-old Nicholas to tidy away his toys, and he was usually quite good at it.

"No. I'll leave them on the floor," he said, "I'll play with them in the morning."

"That's not one of your choices," Annette said. "the floor has to be tidied. If you don't tidy the toys, I'll have to tidy them myself instead of reading you a story."

You could see Nicholas thinking. He looked at his mother intently for a moment, and then continued to play. He played quietly, perhaps hoping his mother would forget. After a while, she took him to his room, settled him to bed, kissed him, and said in a friendly tone:

"I'll go and tidy your toys now, and you can have a story tomorrow night."

Nicholas threw a tantrum and screamed, hoping Annette would change her mind, but she simply left the room. Shortly afterwards, she came back to check on him and found him asleep.

Next day, he made no objections to tidying his toys before bedtime.

"You can clear up your toys now."

Effective and respectful

In this incident, Nicholas had learnt that there were clear boundaries and limits in his world, he had even tested the limits to see if they were firm, and he now felt more secure. **When children know you mean what you say, life is easier and more peaceful all round** – including for themselves.

Annette has not used any of the common ways of 'disciplining' children which hassled parents tend to fall back on – coaxing, bribing, making decisions on the hop, reminding, nagging, making empty threats, shouting, scolding, smacking... What has she done instead? Quite simply, she has offered her son a choice – to tidy up or do without a bedtime story. And she has respected his decision, allowing him to live with the consequences of what he has chosen. **Allowing children to make choices (within limits) and to live with the consequences is a respectful, effective method of discipline.**

This is not the *only* effective and respectful method. We have been learning about effective methods of discipline in every chapter of this book – ignoring some misbehaviours, avoiding unnecessary confrontation, encouraging, listening, making time for guidance, allowing a child to express feelings that are controlling her, giving an I-message, speaking in a respectful, non-aggressive voice – and, possibly most effective of all, making time to pay positive, focused attention to a child. All of these skills are part of good discipline. But parents will not be effective if they do not set *limits* as well as showing affection.

Learning from consequences

That is what is different with this method of discipline. Many parents make threats about what will happen if a child does not go to sleep, does not eat, does not stop squabbling... Quite often, they do not follow through on what they say. They talk, but they do not act! A child quickly learns that he can ignore these empty threats.

When children have to live with consequences, however, they experience the security of firm boundaries; they learn about the real world, and they become more responsible. Adults are constantly learning from consequences: when they overspend, or drink too much, or forget something, or drive carelessly. They learn because they are not protected from consequences. Responsibility increases with practice in making decisions and learning from the good and bad consequences that result. Here is an example.

she decided to taste the sand again

One-year-old Orla enjoys playing in the sandpit her father has made for her outside the back door. When she put some sand in her mouth recently, he lifted her into the house, wiped the sand away, and let her play on the living-room floor, ignoring her tears and screams to get outside. After a minute or so, he carried her to the sand again. She played quietly for a while, then decided to taste the sand again. Within seconds, she was hoisted out of the sand, had her mouth wiped, and again found herself on the floor of the living room. It was five minutes before she was allowed back to the sand this time – and ten minutes the next time. Gradually, she began to get the message that eating sand had unpleasant consequences for her. Babies may not

understand words, but can still learn from the consequences of their choices!

Being removed is a choice

But Orla did not have a choice, you may argue. Her father had removed her from the sand each time without consulting her. This is true. If Orla had been older, it would have been respectful to say, "If you put sand in your mouth again, I'll have to take you inside," but she was too young to understand. Yet, she was learning fast that she *did* have a choice: play in the sand without putting it in your mouth, or else be removed. She was learning this without nagging, scolding, punishing, or any of the other ways in which undue attention is paid to unacceptable behaviour.

We see from this example that **allowing children to live with consequences does not mean allowing them to live with danger to themselves or others.** There is no way you can allow a toddler to learn from the consequences of running across a busy street! Where the safety of your child or other people is concerned, choices may not be practicable – if a child of fifteen months has discovered how to open the garden gate or the baby seat fastener, you have no choice but to find a way of making him safe – perhaps talking with other parents or experimenting until you find a solution. It is important, then, to childproof children's surroundings as much as possible, so that they have a relatively safe area in which to be free to explore and play – that also means you will not be forever saying 'no.' It is impossible, however, to remove all hazards, whether it be the coal bucket or an electric socket or whatever. In these cases, small children can learn from the consequences of a very limited choice – limit your activity or be removed to a playpen or another room! This also applies to any dangerous or anti-social behaviour your child attempts – biting, hitting, spitting, throwing a tantrum in a shop, and so on. A mother in a parent support group told recently of how sobering it was for her son when she removed him from a shop and did not buy him shoes because he had thrown a tantrum to try to persuade her to buy him sandals instead. When she took him back a few days later, he knew what the limits were and did not protest.

Offering choices

The secret of helping children learn from consequences is to **follow through on what you say you will do, to** *act* **more and speak less.** (Many of us pay *attention* to misbehaviour by saying too much and follow through far too little.) Sometimes this will mean removing the child from a dangerous situation so that she learns from the consequences that this behaviour is not acceptable. At other times, it will mean respecting the child's choice not to eat at a particular meal – but following through by not giving him dessert. If you offer a choice, it is important to allow the child to experience the results of his choice. When you say "I'll give it to you when you ask pleasantly," you can then ignore the child's requests until he does speak respectfully or pleasantly. When you say, "The noise is giving me a headache, so if you want to make noise, you'll have to go outside," you will then need to follow through on that if the noise continues, perhaps by offering another choice – "Okay, you have obviously decided you'd prefer to go outside – do you want me to carry you, or will you go yourself?"

Can you see how effective a choice is in winning a child's co-operation? **You can wear yourself out trying to get children to do things until you discover the magic of offering a limited choice.** A choice *involve*s a child because it gives *her* some say in the decisions that affect her. When she is reluctant to get ready for bed, you can say, "Do you want to wear your nightie or your pyjamas?" When he wants to go outside but refuses to put on his coat, you can say, "Do you want to put on your coat and go out to the garden, or do you want to stay inside?" When he wants to take all his toys to his friend's, he may have a tantrum if you say, "You can take only one toy," but he is more likely to be co-operative when you say, "You can take only one toy – do

you want to take your ball or your book?" Similarly, instead of trying to discipline a 'picky' child during a meal, you might serve only a small portion to begin with, involving the child in eating by offering a limited choice *before* the meal – but don't get hooked into widening the choice! "I have sausages, beans and toast. What would you like?" or perhaps, "Do you want a big spoonful of beans or a small spoonful?" You can even involve a child who regularly delays over a choice and keeps you dangling by quietly saying, "If you can't decide quickly, I'll have to decide for you this time." But watch your tone of voice. Don't spoil it all by speaking impatiently!

We'll look at another example.

Dealing with squabbling

Six-year-old Josh Baker and his four-year-old brother, Angelo, squabbled a lot. When they were angry with each other, they nipped and pulled hair and thumped and could be quite violent, though they had never caused any serious injury. Their parents had often 'taken the bait' by paying attention to this misbehaviour, shouting at their children, threatening them, sometimes being drawn into taking sides.

Mr and Mrs Baker now wanted to stop rewarding the squabbling, so they told the boys to settle their own rows in future, and they then ignored fighting unless there seemed to be genuine danger. That had worked. The squabbling continued, but the parents felt more at peace, knowing that squabbling is pretty normal, perhaps even necessary for some children. One day, however, the fighting was serious, things got out of hand, and the parents felt they needed to intervene. The fight had started over who could play with a lorry, so Mr Baker now confiscated the lorry and spoke with them. He was deliberately calm as he spoke, and with no hint of punishment in what he said. "You can have the lorry back as soon as you come to an agreement about sharing it." Faced with the consequence of doing without the lorry, the boys quickly decided who would play with the lorry first.

Using consequences is not punishment

We see from this story that a choice is best presented in a positive, friendly manner – not as a punishment, and not in an aggressive tone of voice. Mr Baker did not speak *negatively* "No – you can't have the lorry until you settle your differences." Instead, he spoke *positively*, using the 'as soon as' approach. In this way, a choice may not even *sound* like a choice: "Yes, you may watch TV as soon as you have tidied away your toys."/ "Yes, you can go out to play as soon as you've said sorry to Jessica."/ "Yes, you can have your dessert as soon as you've eaten three more spoonfuls." These are limited choices, but at least you are not insisting on your own way, and you are giving a child dignity and respect.

It was also important that Mr Baker spoke calmly, for *how* we speak can make all the difference. If children hear an apologetic tone in your voice, that will often provoke further demands as they struggle to find the limits that offer them security. A punishing, aggressive tone, on the other hand, will often provoke a power struggle. **When you speak calmly and confidently, your child will tend to be more accepting.**

"as soon as you come to an agreement"

Another way to make sure that you do not use consequences as punishment is to try, when possible, to **let the consequence flow naturally or logically out of the situation.** If Mr Baker had said, "Right, neither of you will have pocket-money this week," or "Okay, that's it, you're both going to bed earlier tonight," these might have been felt as punishments, because there is no obvious connection between them and the squabbling. Only if the boys had *broken* something should they have had to do without pocket money – in order to *pay* for it. If they had got up at six in the morning, they might have had to go to bed early that evening to make up for their loss of sleep. These would then have been logical consequences of their actions, and not punishments.

Time out

But what would have happened if the two boys had gone off, still angry with each other, and a savage row had broken out? **For extremely disruptive behaviour, parents will occasionally need to use more drastic action – like 'time out.'** In this case, 'time out' might mean separating Josh and Angelo and removing them to somewhere boring to give them a few minutes to cool down and think about what to do instead. 'Somewhere boring' might be just inside the back door and just inside the front door. If you leave one of them in the room where the fight started, that may seem like taking sides.

For a small child, 'time out' usually involves removing him for a few minutes to a room with no distractions (preferably not his own bedroom), or to a special, hard 'time out' chair. There, he has time to think about what is happening. The child will sometimes need to be brought back to the chair as gently and respectfully as possible, even firmly (but again gently) *held* in the chair for the few minutes – and returned to the chair for a longer period if he continues to be disruptive. If he cries, a parent might stay with him, giving good attention (and thus dealing with the underlying cause). All this is demanding on a parent, but 'time out' is so boring for children that they soon learn from the consequences that disruptive behaviour does not pay. It is another example of more action and less talking – but going on about it, preaching or teaching the lesson, may only draw attention to the misbehaviour. It also helps to remember that children are different, so something like 'time out' may help one child to learn but may not help another child.

Talking it out in advance

'Time out' is not recommended as a normal method of discipline – it is only used when things have got completely out of hand – and when you have explained the rules in advance. Indeed, **it helps to talk out *any* form of discipline with children so that you are not reacting on the spot, they know what to expect, and they have time to adjust to the limits.**

When you are under pressure, then, which is when you are most likely to make snap decisions and discipline poorly, you could try withdrawing from a power-struggle and postponing your decision: "I'm not sure what to do about this. I'll have to think about it and talk to you later." That may help you to be more flexible, not just insisting on things because your parents did it this way, or "because I say so." When you have decided on the limits, it is good to give your child *reasons* for them, and *then* to be firm and consistent.

Discipline becomes easier when you have thought about it, talked about it beforehand, and children are prepared. When they know in advance that they will not be taken out shopping the next time if they start screaming for sweets at the cash desk, your trip will be easier. When they know in advance that their playmates will have to leave your house as soon as fighting starts, they soon learn to co-operate.

Taking time to *prepare* children for something will often win their co-operation. Bedtime, for example, becomes a more pleasant routine when you prepare your child for it, maybe an hour

beforehand, by saying something like: "Bedtime is coming soon, so you'll be having a nice warm bath, and then we'll have a story and a cuddle and a lovely rest." When you rush a child, you can easily cause confrontation and upset. It is so much better to say, "We'll be going down town in ten minutes" than to say, "Quickly! Go to the toilet and get your coat on!" Better still if you add something like, "If you're ready in time, we'll be able to visit granny/ feed the ducks." Sometimes, though, preparing is as simple as remembering to bring along a few toys to the dentist's or doctor's waiting room to help your child cope with boredom or anxiety. A gardener knows that the key to success is to prepare the ground well for planting. In the same way, thinking ahead, or preparing children, helping them know what to expect, can make discipline easier – and it lessens the chance that you will end up resorting to emotional or physical abuse.

Self-discipline

That raises the question of *self*-discipline, including controlling your temper and not exposing a young child to strong, scary feelings. This is so important because **disciplining children is all about helping them learn to become self-disciplined,** so that they can increasingly make responsible decisions for *themselves*. A parent's self-discipline provides them with a model.

Self-discipline is also important because offering choices will not work unless *we* have the discipline to be firm and consistent in following through on consequences. That can be difficult. We want to be liked, perhaps to give a child almost everything she wants. We may be nervous of letting her suffer consequences or experience limits. "Let him eat what he likes, and whenever he likes. Let her go to bed when it suits her. Let him watch TV if that's what makes him happy. Give her treats on demand." But this 'no limits' mentality can do damage. **Misbehaviour needs to be interrupted, and mis-behaving children will kick harder and misbehave more in their search for limits**

and firmness. We (and our children) will end up paying for the lack of limits now and in the future unless we are prepared to resist the pressure to be 'nice guy' parents. Isn't it better that your child battles with limits and throws tantrums at the age of three than at forty-three!

Now, no one is totally consistent. Some days, you will feel stressed and under pressure. When you are under the weather or having a bad day, it is okay if you let go of the rules and allow your children to do things you would not normally allow them to do – as long as the general *pattern* is consistent. Being sometimes relaxed about your rules should not be a cause for guilt – parents carry enough guilt already!

'time out'

When others disagree with you
Another place you can model self-discipline is in your relationship with other adults. If you have a partner, or if you live with a parent or in-law, do you take time to talk about who will do what tasks and what you expect of each other? Your planning can include anything from baby-sitting arrangements to the sharing of tasks. There are no rules about what is right for a woman to do, or what is right for a man; what matters is that neither of you is

overburdened or feels hard done by. There is a different atmosphere in a home where these areas of tension are talked out. And it is good for your children to *know* that you talk out limits and rules for yourself.

That is not always easy. Friends, parents, in-laws, or a partner may be uncooperative. How do you cope then? Or when these people disapprove of your methods of discipline? Or when they use methods that threaten to undermine yours? With a little thought and adaptation, however, **all the methods in this course can also work with other adults** – listening, encouraging, not taking the bait, using 'I' messages, using consequences... You can afford to allow a certain amount of leeway to grandparents and others who have a different style to yours. If you are separated, and the children spend weekends with a 'nice' parent who does not set limits, that becomes more difficult. In some cases, you may need to talk to the other parent – though children soon get used to what each parent expects.

In dealing with another adult, as in dealing with a child, you will not always 'win' or get your own way. As you become more comfortable with these skills, and more respectful, however, everyone stands to gain, including yourself. Your confidence will often impress even your critics and leave them more open to you.

Summing up
Discipline is not about coaxing or forcing children to do what we want them to do. It is about helping them learn *self*-discipline, and especially helping them through the rough patches they meet in their development. All the skills in this book contribute to good discipline. They provide children with two great needs: limits on their misbehaviour, and affection. In this chapter we have concentrated on how to help them learn from the consequences of their own choices.

When there is danger, or when the behaviour is totally unacceptable, we may need to remove a child rather than offer a choice – although even here there is scope for limited choices, "Do you want me to carry you, or do you want to go yourself?"

In general, however, it is good to be flexible and not to have too many rules. We avoid humiliating a child or engaging in power struggles by offering a choice. "If you throw bread on the floor again, I'll have to take away your food." This often diffuses a situation and allows a child to keep his dignity by making a different choice. If your two-year-old decides to test the limits, for example by deliberately dropping a piece of bread on the floor after being given a choice, he then experiences the consequences by having the food removed. Tears may follow as he continues to test the limits and see if you will change your mind – but the great thing about offering choices is that there is flexibility, you can usually offer *another* choice, "If you pick up the piece of bread and put it in the kitchen bin, you can have your food back." There is no hint of punishment here. When offering a choice, parents avoid 'punishing' by linking the child's behaviour with a logical or natural consequence, and by speaking in a calm, friendly voice. This is a respectful, effective way of helping children gradually learn self-discipline.

But perhaps the greatest discipline of all is the one we have continually come back to throughout this book – making time for giving positive, loving attention to a child. This 'quality time' has such a powerful effect on children and their behaviour that we will be devoting the next chapter entirely to it.

TABLE 5: DISCIPLINE

*Below are some suggested ways of using consequences, but they are only **suggestions** – each situation and child is different. Note the absence of nagging or scolding. Do any of the examples remind you of situations **you** need to deal with?*

BEHAVIOUR	USING CONSEQUENCES	EFFECT
1. Baby eats sand/ touches electric socket.	Calmly remove to playpen for short time. If behaviour is repeated, leave in playpen for longer time. Remain calm, ignoring tantrum.	Baby learns to play harmlessly, without undue attention.
2. Children squabbling in kitchen.	Offer choice: *Do you want to squabble up in the bedroom or play quietly here?* Then, if necessary: *Do you want me to carry you up to the bedroom, or to go yourselves?...*	Children learn to make choices – and they keep their dignity.
3. Gary won't eat his cereal – he wants toast instead.	You will usually know if this is just attention seeking. If so, say he can have toast when he *finishes* the cereal. No snacks between meals if he doesn't eat – he lives with consequences.	Gary stops using meals as battlefield – and life becomes easier for parents!
4. Imani cries whenever limits are imposed.	It won't usually help to say *Stop crying*. Try comforting her with a hug (but don't push). Be relaxed about tears and *allow* her to cry. Hold to your position, however.	Imani feels security of limits – but also freedom to express feelings.
5. Mary gets up out of bed after you have settled her.	Try: *No bedtime story tomorrow evening if you get up again – you decide.* Or: *Bed earlier tomorrow if you get up again.* But *follow through* on what you say you'll do.	This will often solve the problem – and she learns that you mean what you say.
6. Carlos won't let you brush his teeth.	Offer choice between having teeth brushed and giving up sweet things. He may hold out for a few days until he's convinced you mean it. Avoid any hint of 'punishment.'	Takes responsibility for teeth – and sees link between sweets and tooth decay.
7. Nia doesn't come when called.	Give advance warning – '5 minutes to go.' Then offer choice – "Do you want to come or be carried?" Or "Come in time or do without dinner/ eat it cold." If she throws tantrum, hold her to prevent damage, or remove her to safe room. Try to stay calm.	Nia free to off load feelings – but gets the message. Fewer tantrums – as they no longer work.
8. Jim throws tantrum at supermarket sweet counter.	Parent doesn't give in – or there'll be a successful tantrum at every sweet counter – but Jim is not allowed to go shopping next time unless he agrees to "no sweets."	Jim learns boundaries.
9. Jane leaves her toys scattered on the floor.	She is not allowed her next treat – bedtime story, television, or whatever – until she clears up. (But parent 'helps' her clear up if there are a lot of toys – or very strong objections.)	Jane learns to take responsibility for her own 'mess.'

GETTING IN TOUCH

*Tick any of the situations in Table 5 that remind you of situations that **you** would like to deal with? (If that does not help you to get in touch with a situation, you could also look at the list of behaviours that annoy or upset parents in the Getting in Touch section at the end of chapter one.)*

CASE STUDIES

1. *How would you cope with a child who has started spitting at people? Which of the following choices might work best? Or is there another choice?..*
A. Tell the child, "If you do that again, I'll have to remove you."
B. Tell the child, "If you want to stay here, you can't spit; if you want to spit, you can spit in the washbasin in the bathroom."
C. Ask, "Do you want to say sorry for spitting at George, or do you want to go up to the bedroom?"
D. Ask child "Do you want to leave the room or do you want **me** to remove you?"

2. *Which of the following choices might work for a two-year-old girl who refuses to put on her coat? Would you be prepared to let her live with the consequences?*
A. Tell the child, "If you don't put your coat on, you can't go outside to play.
B. Let her choose for today, and see if she learns from the consequence: "Okay, you don't have to, but it's cold outside, and *I'm* putting on *my* coat."
C. Ask, "Do you want to put on your coat, or will I put it on for you?"

3. *What choices or consequences might be suitable for a behaviour problem **you** have to deal with? – Table 5 may give you some ideas. Can you think of a respectful way of offering the choice? And how might you allow the child to live with the consequences?*

PLANNING

Think of *one* behaviour you need to deal with at present. For a baby, you will not be able to use a choice – you may just need to be gentle but firm about bedtime, baths, nappy-changing, or whatever – but how will you offer an older child a choice, and what consequences might help the child to learn that the limits are to be taken seriously? How could you present this as a *choice* rather than as a punishment? Where and when will you do this? With which child?…

My plans _____

_____

• *Please read chapter six of your handbook before the next session.*

CHAPTER 6: QUALITY TIME

"I don't know what to do. You can't satisfy him. He wants attention all day long. He'd wear you out! As if I didn't have enough to do – I don't have time to breathe! I just don't know how other parents cope…"

A person or a 'chore'?

Nicole, the local health visitor had just dropped in, and Gemma was glad to be able to talk to her about the strain she was under. As she talked, however, it became obvious to Nicole that *Gemma* was the problem, not her three-year-old son, Will. The picture Gemma painted was of a constant round of cleaning, washing, cooking, vacuuming, ironing, tidying... **She was spending her whole life *doing* things for Will – instead of giving him a little of the relaxed, 'noticing' attention he was screaming for.** Much of her tidying was driven by the idea that the house must be as tidy as possible at all times; there were always 'things to be done' rather than a little person to be loved in the present. *He* wanted play and fun and a sense of being loved and special, but she was too preoccupied and driven, too busy 'coping with his demands' in a fixed, patterned way to let go and give him what he needed. No wonder he was demanding.

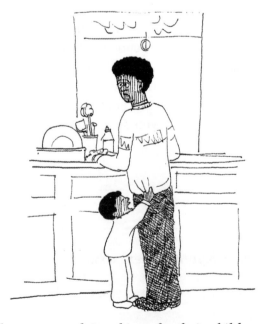

hours spent doing things for their children

Nicole knew there was no point in preaching. Parents have to find their own solutions if they are to become more effective. All she could do was support Gemma by asking questions and making some suggestions. Over a number of weeks, Gemma began to see the difference between positive parenting and *doing* things for Will. That awareness changed her. She began to give him more attention. There was no sudden change, but as she became more relaxed and at ease with Will, he seemed to realise he was important to her, a person rather than a chore or burden, and he became less demanding.

Thirteen minutes a day

Gemma is not unusual. Parents will gladly work long hours of overtime to be able to buy things for their children, they will give hours of their time to doing things *for* their children, but they will sometimes devote only *minutes* to quality time, to being 'present' to a child. Usually this is just a lack of awareness – parents may *think* they spend hours on end with their children, but **a child quickly picks up that other things seem to be more important to mum or dad** – the news on the radio, washing and ironing, a succession of television programmes, cups of tea with a neighbour, cooking and cleaning, paying bills, mending, chatting on the phone, the garden... All these things have their own importance, but it is the lack of balance that can affect a child. Parents sometimes give their children sweets and treats and trips to the cinema and expensive toys – instead of the time and affection they crave. A recent survey shows that fathers spend less than five minutes a day with their children, and this lack of balance applies even to mothers or fathers who stay at home all day to care for their small children – a recent study of six hundred families from different backgrounds found that parents who do not work outside the home only give an average thirteen minutes a day of quality time to their children!

What is this quality time, then, or what does it look like? Here is an example (but it is only *one* example – bear in mind that quality time has more to do with your mentality and your attitude to a child than with any particular set of behaviours).

"I love you as big as the sky"
Emma Hopkins has noticed that her three-year-old son, Christopher, is much more responsive at bedtime than at any other time of the day. It is almost as if he senses her undivided attention and wants to hold onto her a little longer. So this has become Christopher's time for songs, rhymes and stories. He loves the intimacy of being cuddled while they talk together, and he has let her know in different ways that it is his favourite time of day.

The stories Emma reads have their own value, but they are usually only a springboard for their chat together and the more interesting stories 'from her head.' She believes it is also important to *tell* Christopher she loves him, so she makes a point of sometimes ending the bedtime settling with one of her special ways of doing that. Last week, she said, "Who loves you?... And when will I stop loving you?... And can you guess how *much* I love you?... Do you want me to tell you?..." She went on to tell him, "I love you as big as the sky, and all the clouds, and all the stars... as big as a thousand elephants... as big as a hundred mountains... as big as the sea, and all the rivers in the world flowing into it..." Christopher's eyes sparkled.

"I love you as big as the sky"

Attention and touch
Most of us are aware of the importance of stories, rhymes and songs for stretching children's imagination and encouraging language development, but you can imagine how totally different Christopher's experience might be if Emma left a cassette or CD player by his bedside! Television, computers and CD players open up great possibilities for learning, but can never replace personal attention. **Christopher needs this intimacy and touch from a parent in order to develop well emotionally and socially.**

Many parents find, as Emma does, that their children are more responsive at bedtime (though some experts suggest we should avoid talking about anything scary at that time). You will know best what times suit *your* child. Throughout the book, we have seen how good it is for a child to be cuddled close to you at these times. Touch 'notices' and gives positive attention to a child; it builds confidence and self-esteem – an occasional squeeze during the day, a hug, a cuddle, a pat on the shoulder, a kiss, stroking a cheek, holding a hand... Hugs will go much further than scolding in dealing with a child who is jealous of her new brother, for she needs that reassurance that *she* still matters. Virginia Satir, who spent her lifetime studying families and what makes them tick, claims that **children need four hugs a day just to survive** – and more like sixteen hugs a day to grow and blossom and develop good self-esteem. Touch is important to quality time.

Hugs, incidentally, can be two-way, receiving as well as giving. Imagine how your young child may feel if you sometimes say, "I need a hug..." And, after enjoying the hug, you add, "Thanks, that was just what I needed!"

The importance of play
Another major way of giving children quality time is in play. They learn through play. It stretches them. You may never know how much they are benefiting from it – even working off anger by thumping play

dough or a Teddy, or dealing with their nightmares and terrors by being the monster in a game of 'monster-hunt' with you. You might simply fill a basin with water and give them a few empty yoghurt containers or plastic cups. It's a lot easier to wipe a few spills off the kitchen floor than listen to moaning all afternoon. And some of the best toys cost little or nothing – water, sand, dough, used Christmas cards, lids of coffee and jam jars that float in the bathtub, cardboard boxes...

Children *need* to play – sometimes alone, sometimes with others, but also sometimes *along* with you. **When they are playing or amused, parents tend to ignore them; yet their play provides one of the best opportunities for quality time.** We have already seen the value of play-listening, where you quietly join a child at play, inside or outside, in the sandpit, in the bedroom, or at the bathtub. It may help to look more closely at that now.

'Play-listening' again

Take the situation where your daughter spends a long time creating a picture, then scribbles all through it or blotches it with black paint. You may feel like saying "Oh, your lovely painting! Why did you do that?" But that is looking at her play from an adult point of view. With play-listening, you merely *notice* what she does, "You're scribbling with the black now." In that way she feels accepted and valued by you. You are respecting her need to be creative in her own unique way.

children need to play

The trouble with play-listening is that, when you try it, it feels boring and unproductive to just *watch* a child and only make an occasional noticing comment. (This applies particularly to fathers, who usually want to be active.) There may be no immediate spin-off, and your presence does not seem to make much difference. It may be a number of weeks, even months, before you see the benefits in the improved relationship with your child (or a lessening in misbehaviour). Yet this is true quality time, and possibly the most significant skill on the course.

'Play-listening,' however, is only one way to be with children at play. There will be other times when your play-time will be anything but quiet – special fun-times when you make time to play *with* them. So here is another 'quality time' example:

A 'fun-dad' for his daughters

Gordon McPherson is a 'fun-dad' for his two daughters, Debbie (6) and Lisa (2). It is obvious that he *enjoys* them – and that the girls love him. Since they were a few months old, he loved to play peekaboo, round-and-round-the-garden, pat-a-cake, this little piggy... Six-year-old Debbie still loves to play 'baby' things like pat-a-cake occasionally for the special attention it gives her. Why not? But now it is mostly hide-and-go-seek, or 'wrestling' with them on the carpet, or baffling them with one of the three magic tricks he has learned to do. On a Saturday morning he sometimes likes to surprise them with, "What will we do today?" and he goes with their suggestions. On a recent Saturday, when Debbie answered, "We'll have a picnic in the park," Gordon did not protest. He did not point out that it was raining (and the middle of winter!) or say that he had a better idea. Instead, he let Debbie prepare the picnic with him, and off they went to the park. After eating a sandwich in the rain, he asked, "What will we do now?" and Debbie replied, "We'll run up and down the hill." They ran up and down the hill. "What will we do next?" Gordon asked. "Run up and down again" was the immediate reply.

Up and down they ran until they were both exhausted. "Children amaze me," he remarked, afterwards, "In a million years I would never have imagined this was what Debbie would have wanted to do... It's a lot more bother, but it's fascinating when you let *them* lead."

a 'fun dad' for his daughters

Being playful is a decision
For some parents, this kind of playfulness can be an escape; they may be playful and full of fun for their children but grumpy and uncooperative with a partner. Gordon is not like that. He decided some time ago that being playful is a decision you can make. "My family needs me to be good-humoured," he claims, "I can't afford the luxury of being down-hearted – they need me to brighten up and be cheerful and playful. But I talk about heavy things somewhere else – otherwise I'd be false."

Not many of us, perhaps, could measure up to this ideal or let go of the controls to this extent, but it is nice to meet someone like Gordon who can show us what is possible and inspire us to *enjoy* our children more and bring more fun and good humour into their lives. For those of us who feel a bit stuck, even depressed by how far we are from that ideal, some parent organisations suggest that we plan to spend even one session of *twenty* continuous minutes a week with each of our children, giving them special attention, perhaps taking them out of the house to a park or to

some place that's different, but doing what the children *themselves* want. This needs to be done freely and cheerfully, however – with no correcting or warning or scolding for those twenty minutes.

Twenty minutes a week per child?
Twenty minutes of 'special time' may seem very little. You may want to object that parenting is not about scheduling a fixed time in the week for your child! But **having a limited 'special time' is a great way to build lasting memories for young children and it has been found to improve the whole quality of parenting for the rest of the week.** Setting aside 'special time' changes parents. They learn a lot about parenting as opposed to *doing things* for their children. Children, too, pick up the vibes that you are more relaxed and available to talk to, open to listening, ready (within limits) to let go and have fun. And they may keep coming to you when they are adolescents.

Other parents may have the opposite objection. They feel burdened and pressured by the suggestion of 'special time,' especially if they have a number of young children. But **individual one-to-one quality time may be even *more* necessary if you have a number of children.** Much squabbling, for example, arises out of jealousy and the 'displaced' child's sense that he is no longer special to you. 'Special time' may be just what he needs.

Some guidelines for 'special time.'
Based on years of experience, The Parents' Leadership Institute of Palo Alto offers some guidelines for this 'special time' with a child. One guideline is that you be open, as far as possible, to doing **whatever the *child* wants you to do for that time** (if your baby is too young to talk, watch her and she will 'tell' you what she wants.) This does not mean allowing your children to do whatever they wish at *other* times – we have seen how important firm limits can be – so allowing them to choose how they want to have fun applies particularly to your special fun-times in the week. They

will often surprise you with what they want to do. Sometimes you will need to make suggestions to widen their experience, so you can surprise *them* – when you put a carrier seat on your bicycle and ask where they want to go, or you ask if they would like to look for acorns or leaves or wild flowers to bring home, or you offer them a window sill or a tiny patch of your garden, and ask what they would like to grow. As you can imagine, this is not an easier way to be a parent – but there is a huge pay-off!

A second guideline for 'special time' is that we give up the huge advantage we have in size and strength and experience. Adults may not realise how big they seem to their children, and what an unfair advantage they start with, so you are asked to **consider not *tickling* a child**, certainly not putting the child into a helpless state of being tickled. Tickling puts you even more in control, and may be meeting your needs rather than the child's. On a similar note, you might avoid being competitive. That means playing for fun, not to win (again, this may be harder for dads than mums!) When you do play ball games or board games that are competitive, you will need to give up your advantage and **lose most of the games**, but not all the time. It is best not even to say something like, "Oh, drat, you're winning again!" because that says winning is important.

or a tiny patch of your garden

Two hours to clean the house!

We began with the story of Gemma who was too busy doing things for her son to give him the attention and quality time he was screaming for. But there is someone else who is screaming for quality time and attention. Yourself. Recently, a parent in one of our support groups said, "I have two hours to clean the house while he's at the crèche." Then she heard what she had just said. To clean the house! Not to go for a swim, or walk in the fresh air in a park, or listen to her favourite music, or sit down with her feet up to read a magazine, or have a cuppa with a friend, or take a much needed nap, or relax in the way she most enjoyed relaxing...

So what about *you*? How do you make space for yourself? How often do you have an evening out with a partner or with friends? (It is often said that the best thing parents can do for children is to love their partners.) When do you have time to play and have some fun? Do you tell someone when *you* need a hug? In what five or six ways do you *like* to relax – and how long is it since you relaxed in some of these ways?

In your circumstances, all this may be difficult, but what about finding someone in a similar situation to your own and making some arrangement like swapping baby-sitting? You will need to find a *balance* between your child's need for quality time and your own, but **you owe it to yourself and your children to find space for things that renew and relax you.** That may mean saying a firm 'no' to the guilt feelings that arise. It may also mean settling for being what Dr Donald Winnicott calls a 'good enough' parent rather than a perfect one.

Summing up

To sum up. Parents often work tirelessly for their children or spend long hours in the same house as them without being *present* to them. They wonder why the child is 'acting up' when he is really screaming for the attention and quality time that is not being given.

Quality time takes various shapes, but it

involves many of the things we have been learning about in this book – listening, touch, talking, being playful, watching our body language and tone of voice... It may involve very simple things like walking the dog with dad or mum in the early morning, or 'helping' you with the gardening. Or it may mean snatching moments of the day to chat and cuddle, or joining a child at play to notice or play-listen for a few minutes. One concrete way of giving quality time is to plan even one period of twenty minutes a week 'special time' with each child, when you are open to doing whatever the child most wants. In later years, this may develop into a weekly 'family meeting' as described in our publication "What can a parent do?" One way or another, a weekly 'special time' is a powerful way to keep alive for many years what you are learning on this course.

'Special time' is not a matter of what you *do* with a child. It is more a question of *how* you spend this time, and of the patience and kindness that go with positive parenting. At times, that may call for more courage and self-discipline than you can muster, so do go easy on yourself. Settle for being less than perfect. You'll never get it all together!

Keeping the balance

Throughout the book, we have seen how important limits and affection are. They need to be balanced. Clear limits provide the background against which quality time

misbehaviour lessens when he feels loved

makes sense. You will need to be reasonably consistent in sticking to the limits you set and not give in to your child or be too quick to offer help. In chapter five, we saw that offering choices is a respectful way to set these limits: it encourages co-operation instead of provoking a reaction or a tantrum.

That said, there is a sense in which this chapter on 'quality time' brings everything else in the book together – including how you deal with misbehaviour. You build a bond with your child and nourish her growth and self-esteem when you pay less attention to misbehaviour and spend quality time with her. Because she feels encouraged and loved and special to you, you will probably notice that misbehaviour lessens at other times – she does not have the same need to scream for your attention. In her excellent book, *The Magic of Encouragement,* Stephanie Marston states, **"When our kids can count on us to give them focused attention, many problems melt away."**

Go gently

Change will not normally happen overnight. Parenting skills are learnt with practice and *patience.* Some parents like to do the course a second or even a third time, perhaps zoning in on a different child each time. Others move on to another community programme that reinforces the same skills. Others make huge strides when they *lead* a course. Some simply continue to read a chapter of this book each week and plan around it. In these ways, their learning goes on and their journey in parenting becomes more rewarding. For no matter how important your other work may be, there is probably no greater contribution you can make, no more worthwhile task you can perform, than to work at improving communication in your family. Besides, many parents tell us that these skills turn out to be useful in all sorts of other situations – at home, at work, or in the community.

Good luck on your journey, then, and happy parenting. And go gently!

TABLE 6: QUALITY TIME

Which two areas below have you tended to neglect, and which two areas have you been reasonably good at?

ACTIVITY	HOW IT WORKS
1. HAVING FUN AND GAMES TOGETHER	Both Dads and Mums create happy memories and security for their children when they make time for fun, sometimes as a family and sometimes on a one-to-one basis – even twenty minutes a week for each child. For this 'special time,' it may be best not to tickle, to take the emphasis off winning or losing, and to let the *child* take the lead in deciding what to play – for babies, watch and you'll see.
2. STORIES, SONGS AND RHYMES	When a child sits cuddled into a parent, listening to or reading stories, followed by a chat together, she is not just being 'stretched,' having her imagination, intelligence and language development fed – her sense of security and values are also being formed, and her emotional development is thriving. (Television is good, but can never replace all that for a child.)
3. 'NOTICING' CHILD AT PLAY – WITH WATER, SAND, TOYS..	Children develop through play – even with a simple basin of water and empty yoghurt containers on the kitchen floor. Watch for interest so that you avoid 'pushing' with unsuitable toys, but, above all 'notice' the play. 'Noticing' includes listening, looking, showing an interest, and generally giving good attention when it is *not* being demanded. You might join a child at play, forget about 'helping,' supervising, or even suggesting, and just enjoy watching quietly – with an occasional comment that *reflects* what you see.
4. 'NOTICING' CHILD WITH SMILES, HUGS, KISSES, TOUCHING.	Show affection regularly. It is said that <u>all</u> children need at least four hugs a day to *survive*, and sixteen a day to *thrive!* Cuddling, smiling, touching say, *You are good; you are loveable; you are beautiful.* You might cuddle in closely for reading a story, or get down on the ground and let your baby crawl over you.
5. LOOKING AFTER YOURSELF	Plan 'quality time' for yourself too. You have more to give your child when you've taken exercise and fresh air, and when you have relaxed, done something you enjoy, laughed, and had some fun. Planning for yourself includes planning time with a partner and/ or adult friends (even joining a parent and toddler group). Remember that children learn a great deal about love and life from watching adult relationships.

CASE STUDIES

*Some of the comments below are parent's questions, suggestions, corrections or opinions – rather than simply saying what the parents **notice** or how they feel. **These comments may be quite appropriate at times**, but there are special benefits to a child when a parent just **notices** ('play-listens') or speaks feelings (an 'I-message') and doesn't suggest or ask or offer an opinion.*

    A. *Do you agree with the way the comments are labelled in column 1 below?*

    B. *Can you help each other label the comments in column 2 in a similar way?*

Column 1: MAKING A PICTURE

1. Mm. That's a very pretty picture you're making. (**Opinion**)
2. Mm. You're making a picture. (**Noticing**)
3. Mm... What are you drawing? (**Question**)
4. There's too much black in the picture. (**Correction**)
5. I love watching you. (**I-message**)
6. Would you like to colour in the sky?... (**Suggestion**)
7. You're making the picture greener now. (**Noticing**)
8. You're a brilliant artist! (**Opinion**)
9. That's three flowers you've made. (**Noticing**)
10. I like that colour. (**I-message**)
11. Who's the funny man in the middle? (**Question**)
12. Now you're using the yellow... (**Noticing**)

Column 2: PLAYING WITH WATER

1. You've got both hands in the water.
2. Watch you don't spill it.
3. It's nice for me to be here.
4. Why don't you put your fish in?
5. That's two things you've put in the boat.
6. Mm. You're washing Teddy's face.
7. Mm. Give Teddy a drink while you're at it.
8. Don't be selfish – move over and let Tim play too.
9. No! You're not allowed to drink the water.
10. Oh. You're splashing the water... Splash!... Splash!
11. I like the way you make the duck float.
12. You've decided to dry Teddy.

PLANNING AHEAD

1. How do you feel about joining a child at play, even for a few minutes, this week? Which child? Where? When? What might you need to be careful about? Parents of babies might set aside some time to do nothing but relax and enjoy the baby.

My plans _____

*2. How will you make time to look after **yourself** this week? – Make a 'date' with your partner? Make time for exercise, fresh air, reading, or something you enjoy?*

My plans _____

> • *If you are attending the optional seventh session on a child's spiritual development, please read the corresponding chapter in the appendix.*

APPENDIX: YOUR CHILD'S SPIRITUAL DEVELOPMENT
(This chapter is part of an optional additional session for parents interested in this topic.)

pushed him onto the grass and sat on him

Not like the book said

It was Saturday. The morning when Tim usually gave special time to his five-year-old stepdaughter, Aileen. They walked to a local park. Under the wooden bridge in the playground Tim became a troll, and Aileen squealed with delight each time she escaped across the bridge. Then, she chased him around a tree until she caught him, pushed him onto the grass and sat on him – she could be quite aggressive! Next, they picked a bunch of daisies, dandelions and buttercups to bring home. She knew the names of these flowers, but, when he asked her to name them, she refused, saying, "You're asking me too many questions!"

After an hour, they headed for home. They had had some close moments, but for most of the time, Aileen had been in a grumpy mood, hard to satisfy, unco-operative. Tim felt discouraged. Quality time wasn't like the book said!

"I'm really tired," he told his wife. "I mean, I like being with her in small doses, but it's demanding. She takes all your energy, doesn't she..."

Next morning at church did not help. The minister talked about how Christians are called to give everything, to hold nothing back – and to be rooted in a life of prayer. It was all about what people were neglecting to give and to do, nothing about how much they were *already* giving and

doing, and it made Tim feel bad, guilty, unacceptable. He was not measuring up to God's will for him. He was neglecting so much. It was hard to be a parent and to be spiritual...

A common misunderstanding

This false distinction between daily living and spirituality is not unusual. Many good parents share Tim's misunderstanding and live with considerable guilt because they see themselves not measuring up to their religious ideals. They often feel like second-class citizens in their church. "Others may sell all and give to the poor, but not us," they think, "but we scarcely have the time even to pray." These parents do not realise that **to keep on loving through the daily stresses and strains of family life, sometimes even with a deep sense of failure, is at the very heart of their holiness.** How differently God thinks from they do. If God were to speak with them, they might hear how much they have given up without realising it, and how they have indeed sold all and given to the poor. "When did we do these things?" they might ask in surprise. And they would hear something like this (the following passage is one of the optional religious reflections which may be read aloud during the early part of the course):

Thank you

I was a stranger and you welcomed me. A homeless stranger, and you welcomed me into your home. In spite of the enormous upset I caused to your life and household, you were actually delighted to share your home with me, and you made me welcome. Thank you.

I was naked and you clothed me. I was born completely naked into this world and you wrapped me in little sheets and blankets, and then babygros, and then more clothes, and more clothes. And you washed and ironed and folded those clothes hundreds and hundreds of times. And you've never stopped clothing me, although sometimes you've had to do without things you'd have liked for yourself. Thank you.

I was hungry and thirsty... And you gave me food, and you gave me to drink – Mum, you even wanted to give me the warm milk from your own breasts – and you got quite handy with the bottle, Dad. Again and again and again you fed me, and every time you gave me food you were giving it to me, to Christ. And I appreciated the sacrifices you had to make to feed me, and the boredom of constantly cleaning up the mess I made, and washing and drying an endless pile of dishes after I had eaten, and I am deeply grateful to you. Thank you.

I was sick. With teething and wind, with bouts of 'flu and temperatures and measles and chicken pox and constant colds. And you comforted me, and you lost your sleep, and you were anxious and worried and suffered along with me and stayed off work and cared for me, and I experienced you at your loving best, tender and caring and full of compassion for me. And I knew then how unconditional your love was when I was at my most helpless, and I thought to myself. "Who else would love like this, so selflessly and with such self-sacrifice!" I love you for that. Thank you.

I was in prison. In the prison of my own immaturity, resisting limits, acting up, throwing tantrums. And you didn't just visit me – you came and stayed with me, imprisoning and tying yourself up – for years – for my sake, so you could lead me out into freedom and maturity and an enjoyment of the wonders of life. That freedom was perhaps the greatest gift of all you gave me. How can I say thank you for it?

You have done so much for me. Over and over and over again, even when you were bored or exhausted, irritated or hurt, when you were ill or wanted to count the cost, you forgave me, and you didn't count the cost. You loved me, and I will not ever forget you for it. I want you to know that.

I'm telling you now so you'll be more aware of the good you're doing – and so

you'll know you're doing all this to me, to Christ. And I'm telling you so you'll know how much I appreciate and love you. Thank you...

Parenting and spiritual development

For you as a parent, then, loving your family is something deeply spiritual. Family spirituality is not something you need to *start*. You are already living a spiritual life far more fully than you may realise – even when your marriage or family life seems to be coming apart at the seams! God does not look for results or success. You are merely being invited to work at your close relationships, and to put more effort into that than into anything else. That, for a parent, is selling all and giving to the poor – for the poor, Mother Teresa points out, are in your own home, hungry for your listening, hungry for your eyes and ears and hands, hungry for your encouragement, your touch, your values, your limits, your affection...

The kind of parenting children receive has a *lot* to do with their spiritual development. Their experience of a loving, affectionate, listening parent helps them form their image of a loving God. A child's experience of a parent who allows her to make choices and live with consequences can teach her about a God who is so respectful of her free will that she is allowed to make mistakes. Putting your arms around a crying child and allowing him to express his feelings (instead of saying "don't cry!") may be preparing him for a God who will always allow him, now and as an adult, to express resentment and grief and anger in his prayer – as well as positive feelings. Can you see how much a child is learning about God when you say something like: "I love you, Emily, even when you do things you know you shouldn't." or "I didn't mean to hurt you – I'm sorry I said that!"

Once you become aware that a child's spiritual development is rooted in the ordinary, human events of every day, and that it is not some otherworldly thing, you can begin to think about practical steps for building on the solid foundation you have already been laying. What will help?

A sense of wonder
One thing is to **help introduce small children to the wonders around them and be grateful to God for them** – as long as you do not overdo the *God* angle, making it heavy or unnatural. It may simply be a matter of pointing out trees, flowers, seashells, animals, birds, admiring the shapes and colours, touching them, helping your child to appreciate how things look and smell and sound and feel. Occasionally, as you talk (and listen to a child talk) about these things, you might express your genuine sense of thanks or praise for what you experience, perhaps at that time, or perhaps that evening as a bedtime prayer.

introduce them to the wonders around them

Their deeper questions
Linked with this sense of wonder that comes so naturally to children are the questions they ask, including their most 'difficult' questions: Why is there a moon? Why do birds fly? Why did the birdie die? Did God want it to die? Is God older than granny? How did God start? Do babies get out through their mummies' belly buttons? How do they get inside? Where was I before I was born? What was in the world before God?

Sometimes we dismiss these questions with pat answers, as adults often do when they have stopped asking more basic questions themselves. Or we laugh at the questions and think them silly or strange, perhaps because we have lost our own sense of wonder and may need to re-learn it from a child. Or we answer the child's questions with doctrine, with what is 'right' or 'wrong,' thus giving the false impression that faith is about 'doctrine' rather than a relationship with a loving God – which right and wrong flow out of.

Isn't it so much better to stop and *think* about their questions, and hear the depth and sense of wonder and enquiry that is there? **When you explore a question with your child, or even say you do not know the answer, you allow the child to continue to wonder;** you do not close the questions down as adults closed them down for many of us. See what a different understanding of God and faith emerge when the child gets the message that these questions are open for discussion, do not have clear-cut answers, need to be explored and understood at different stages in our lives and have different answers at different times.

Stories and spiritual development
Stories, too, and the two-way chat that develops around them, are a great way of feeding a child's religious imagination and teaching him to listen. (Learning to listen may be important in helping him learn to pray eventually.) All kinds of stories help, but those published by religious publishers can have special value. Fortunately, there is a steady improvement in the quality of such books, for example from the Lutterworth Press and Scripture Union. There are a number of good, practical suggestions about what to read (and lots more to think about) in a fresh, up to date, little book, "Praying with Sticky Fingers," by Helen Albans (see recommended reading, at the back of this publication).

Stories also help to form children's values and give them a sense of *belonging* to a faith community – stories of the saints and heroes of your church, and especially stories from the Bible. You should not have much difficulty in picking a children's Bible that suits you from the many available (the Fount Children's Bible, for example, makes the stories fascinating, and grabs a child's imagination).

The most interesting stories for a child, however, are about herself – and about you. They can also introduce her to the notion of life as a journey in faith: "When I was small, I used to steal biscuits from the tin in the kitchen – are you surprised?... What do you think of that?..." "When I look back over my life, I can see that God cared a lot about me during difficult times, for example when..." Better still when you can link your own stories with stories from the Bible, "Sometimes I feel like that blind man, and I need to ask God to help me to see..."

_____

At the end of the story I said, "Life was pretty hard for Abraham at times" I was about to say more when she interrupted me, "Life is hard for me too," she said. And out came all her troubles about her friends and who didn't like her and what they had said. This must be what they mean about linking your own story to the Bible story!

_____

In-home rituals
Another way of supporting children on their spiritual journey is with little in-home rituals. 'Rituals' are often thought of as dead practices. That is not what we mean. There is a new appreciation today for family rituals, customs and celebrations that remain fresh and alive. This is something we can learn from the Jewish people who have been sharing and communicating their faith with dynamic rituals for thousands of years. **Rituals are perhaps the most powerful way to make God a natural part of daily family living.** These can include the milestones of the church's year, buying a hyacinth (or better still, a cactus) at the beginning of Lent to flower at Easter, or setting up an empty crib on the first Sunday of Advent, adding the straw on the second Sunday, the animals on

the third Sunday, and so on. Rituals also help us to celebrate and remember together the *family* milestones, the new beginnings, birthdays, a pet's death, anniversaries..

One of the commonest rituals in families is having a special meal together. Most people celebrate birthdays or family occasions with a meal. With a little thought, a meal (perhaps one each week) can be changed from a 'grab and run' affair to become a special family occasion. With a baby, you will feel limited in what you can do, but small children quickly take to and appreciate the sense of occasion when you slow down for a meal and do some of the following things: turn off the TV and play relaxing music; place on the table a few daisies or wild flowers they have helped you pick; light a candle; hold hands as a sign of unity as you thank God before you eat; plan some questions or stories to make the conversation more interesting.

The grace
What grace will you say before (or after) you eat? There is a lot to be said for not rattling off the same fixed prayer every time, or it may become an empty formula. Sometimes it helps to ask: "I wonder what each of you is happy about that you'd like to thank God for?..." At other times, silence may be the best way to have a sense of the presence of God: "Let's take a moment of silence to thank God for this food and for each other."

Blessing a child
In-home rituals also allow you to begin praying with small children long before they can talk. Right from the day their baby comes home from hospital, some parents like to pray over her, either at the baby's or their own bedtime (insofar as a baby does have a bedtime!) Some parents like to touch each child's forehead (or make the sign of the cross on it) as they bless them at this special time each evening – God certainly never meant 'blessings' to be the special reserve of church ministers. On occasions, the touching can be with water, as a reminder of baptism, or with perfumed

oil (like Lavender Oil or moisturising cream), as a sign of the healing love of God. And your prayer can be as simple as: "May God bless you and strengthen you in love and faith through my love and example." As children get older, this prayer over them in the evening is something that can continue, each parent taking time, perhaps, **to pause and look at the sleeping child and bring their concerns about him before God.** Some parents find this the most meaningful prayer in their entire day.

Prayer and vegetable soup

But what can you do to introduce small children to prayer? This is a concern for parents who feel ill at ease with prayer, may not have prayed much for years, and are beginning to rethink their values now that they have children of their own. You may feel unsure about how to pray, or stuck in patterns of prayer that have not changed since you were a child, or you may be dissatisfied with the kind of prayer that is little more than a 'list' – "God bless Mum and Dad and Gran and Kate and Rover..."

Here is a flexible, up to date approach, which may work for both you and your child at different levels. We'll listen to one parent's experience of using it first:

their experience of a loving parent...

"*The Reception Class parents were invited to the school for a talk on praying with our 4 to 5-year-olds. One suggestion was to come together at the children's bedtime, when each of the family might give one example of how they had shown love to someone that day, and thank God for that goodness in themselves; then we might give one example of how we had not shown love, and ask forgiveness for that. We started the next evening. My husband, Steven, said he had smiled at people that day, and he thanked God for that. I couldn't think of a single loving thing I had done, but then I remembered that Louise had asked me to make a jigsaw with her, and I had got up from the TV without complaining. Would the children like to tell us when they had shown love? Not a word! So we went on. Steven said he was sorry for shouting at me that morning, and he kissed me. Not the kind of prayer I was used to, but I was beginning to see the point. I said I had been grumbling and in bad form, and I was sorry now, and I asked each one to forgive me. Now the children's turn. Did they think we had gone mad? We coaxed them, but still nothing. So we said a short prayer of sorrow to God.*"

"*Next evening, it was the same story. And the next. Not a word from the children. It didn't seem to be working for us. Until Louise (5) came in, strong on her good points, not so open about her weaknesses. But she was talking. From then on, the children's response improved. David (3) chipped in with the most complicated story of how everyone else had been naughty and he had been good!*"

"*I don't think I'm exaggerating when I say that this kind of prayer has changed our family life. The children see us now as human, needing their forgiveness. And they can come to us and admit their failings. Even 'serious' things have tumbled out in those end-of-day sessions, and all kinds of things have cropped up that we might never have known about each other – like when I said I had shown love by making vegetable soup for them and Louise said she had shown love when she ate it!*"

stories about herself and about you

Introducing family prayer

Can you see how much the children in this example are learning about what it means to love and not to love, and about right and wrong – but in a context of love and relationships? Nor are they being made to feel shame and guilt; they are being taught to reconcile and to become aware of their *goodness*. They are also learning a lot about God – that God's goodness is working within them, that all goodness comes from God, that God constantly loves and forgives us.

You may like to consider introducing some kind of simple, 'sharing' prayer like this. You do not have to wait until you are going to church on Sundays or until you 'know how to pray' before you start. It is probably most natural when a child is cuddled close to you before bedtime. Music and a candle can sometimes help to create atmosphere. As your child gets older, the prayer might include:
1) thanking God for specific things and people that affected you today, or for God's goodness in yourself today;
2) saying sorry for ways you failed to show love (it is up to themselves to acknowledge their little lapses when they feel able to do so, but others should not remind them of these lapses); and
3) praying for those you care about.

Family prayer does not have to happen every evening. If you decide you want to try it just once a week, it may help to decide on a particular evening in the week, perhaps Saturday or Sunday. If you decide you want to try it each evening you will need to vary the questions to avoid boredom, e.g., two things that happened today that I'd like to thank God for (even that I was able to get up out of bed this morning), or things I saw today – the lovely flowers we saw when we were out walking, things I touched today, smelt today, tasted today, heard today. Or, "What did I not like about today, and did I act on my feelings or show love?" Or, "One of my best ever experiences of God's beauty in people was..." Or, "One of my best experiences of God's beauty in nature was..." Whatever you try, you will certainly have to adapt and be flexible – a method of prayer that suits your small children will hardly be suitable for the same children as they grow older!

Bringing small children to church?

You may wonder how your church fits into all this, if you belong to one – particularly if your circumstances make church attendance difficult while your children are small. When possible, however, and when the service is suitable, and welcomes children, there is much to be said for allowing small children to take part in community and church activities. **Both you and your child *need* support from a faith community.** This also introduces him into an *adult* (or *all-age*) community, and religion is not then something to be shed when he comes of age

Your own lifestyle

Unfortunately, the measure in some churches for being a practising, committed Christian is whether you attend church on Sunday rather than how you live and love in your daily life. Isn't that, perhaps, what matters most in fostering your child's spiritual development? Children learn what they see modelled. They learn about life from how you spend your time and money, how you treat those close to you, especially a partner, if you have one, and how you talk to and about others. They learn to respect and value people when they see you giving them time and respect. They learn to forgive when they experience your forgiveness, "I was angry with you, because that hurt me, but I forgive you." They learn to listen when they are listened to "You hit him? Mm – tell me more... And how do you feel now about that?..."

What they learn is reinforced when you explain *why* you act as you do. See the values you communicate in: "I bought this for Mum because I love her."/ "Yes, he's grumpy, but I think I can understand that – he's lonely."/ "When I walk near the sea, I think how beautiful God must be to make all this."

But children are not the only ones who are learning – you will also be learning along with them, your image of God changing, as your child slows you down and helps you to see things through her eyes and perhaps rediscover the sense of wonder you had when you were a child. This growth in your own faith can also be nourished by reflecting on the events of your life and by making some time for personal prayer. All through this book, there has been emphasis on the importance of making time for yourself; reflection and prayer is another way in which you can nourish and refresh yourself in a way that allows you to love your children (and yourself) more effectively.

touching each child on the forehead

Summing up

In this chapter, we have seen how much we are already doing for our children's spiritual development, perhaps without realising it. **Your most important contribution will continue to be in the ordinary, everyday living and loving of family life.** You may be surprised that some of the suggestions in this chapter are about ordinary, everyday things. They may even seem to draw you closer to each *other* than to God. But holiness, after all, is about loving *one another* as Christ loved us. It is often overlooked that this love is at the centre of all spirituality.

We have explored some ways of building on what you have been doing. Fostering, and learning from, your children's sense of wonder. Dealing respectfully with their questions. Feeding their religious imagination with stories. Making time for meaningful little in-home rituals – meals, blessings, the ritual of a regular prayer time with a child. And we have looked at some ways of starting to pray with children and perhaps introduce them into your own faith community. All these are possible ways, not only of encouraging children's *spiritual* development, but also their physical, emotional, and intellectual development as well. Today we are increasingly aware that each contributes to the other.

Other world faiths

Most church-going people in Britain and Ireland belong to a Christian faith community, so this chapter has been written from a Christian viewpoint, but we are assured that almost all the ideas in it apply to other world faiths. Their spirituality, too, is rooted in everyday human relationships.

At the end of each session of the programme, Muslims following this course are also offered an Islamic reflection, which links the theme of the session with their own religious beliefs and traditions. A similar dimension will be provided for other world religions if there is a demand for it.

TABLE 7: YOUR CHILD'S SPIRITUAL DEVELOPMENT

Here are some things parents have found helpful for young children's spiritual development. There is some overlap, but which do you think might be most important?

SOME IDEAS...	...AND HOW THEY WORK
1. GOOD PARENTING – listening, affection, choices and consequences, responsibilities..	The kind of parenting children receive has a *lot* to do with their spiritual development. Their experience of a loving, affectionate, listening parent helps them form their image of a loving God. You can surprise them with a statement like: *"I love you, Emily, even when you do very naughty things."* or *"I didn't mean to hurt you – I'm sorry I said that."*
2. HOW YOU LIVE AT HOME – how you treat your family, especially your partner, if you have one.	How you treat your family speaks louder than anything you say, for children learn what they see modelled. They learn to forgive, to listen and to love when they see and experience *your* forgiveness, listening and love. *"I was angry with you, because that hurt me, but I forgive you."/ "You hit him? Mm – tell me more... And how do you feel now about that?..."*
3. SHARING YOUR VALUES – saying (and showing) what is important to you, and why.	What you do can be more powerful when you explain *why* – instead of taking it for granted that your children *know* why: See the values you communicate in: *"I bought this for Mum because I love her."/ "Yes, he's grumpy, but I think I can understand that – he's lonely."/ "When I walk near the sea, I think how beautiful God must be to make all this."*
4. STORIES – including your own story, your child's story, and Bible stories.	Stories, and the two-way chat that develops around them, are a great way of developing religious imagination and communicating values. *"When I was small, I used to steal biscuits from the tin in the kitchen – are you surprised?... What do you think of that?..."/ "When I look back over my life, I can see that God cared a lot about me during difficult times, for example when..."*
5. RELIGIOUS PRACTICES – especially within the home.	Little rituals are a powerful way to make God a natural part of daily family living – blessing your baby prayerfully each night, thanking God before you eat, celebrating birthdays/ family occasions... *"Let's take a moment of silence to thank God for this food and for each other."*
6. PRAYER WITH YOUR CHILD – simple, natural, but sincere, avoiding 'babyishness.'	This is probably most natural when a child is cuddled close to you before bedtime. As children get older, it can include: 1) thanking God for specific things and people, 2) saying sorry for ways you failed to show love, and 3) praying for those you care about. Music and a candle sometimes help.
7. SERVICE TO OTHERS – when it flows out of caring.	It is good for children to have some experience of parents whose doors and hearts are open to others beyond the immediate family. Family *unity* on its own may not be enough.
8. A GROWING ADULT FAITH – nourished by life events and prayer.	You will have more to give your child when you are growing in your own life of faith and prayer – partly due to your children and to reflection on the events of your life, partly by making time for personal prayer, especially with scripture.

DISCUSSION

Beside each of the following questions, put the letter Y (for Yes), N (for No), or U (if you are Unsure). Then chat in pairs about how you marked them. This is a listening exercise, not an argument, so please listen with understanding and respect when someone differs from you – you can learn a lot that way!

Is it okay to say to a child, "God loves you, no matter what you do"?
Is it okay to say to a child, "Don't do that! God's looking at you"?
Is a holy person one who prays a lot?
Being holy is all about how you spend your time with those closest to you – true?
Is there any point in praying with children if you don't pray yourself?
Are children naturally loving and good?
Should a pre-school child be punished for telling lies or stealing?
What a child *most* needs from a parent is good example – is that true?
Is the old saying true that 'a family that prays together stays together'?
Is eating together as a family important for a child's spiritual development?

PLANNING AHEAD

Which one thing in Table 7 would you like to build into your life? What will you do this week to introduce that? When? (For example, is there a regular day of the week that might suit?) Where? Who with?...

My plans _____

_____

FURTHER READING

Rather than overawe you with an extensive reading list, we recommend here just a small number of books on parenting young children. Many of the studies mentioned in this book are reported in greater detail or referenced in the books below. For those of you who want to read more, some of these books also have much fuller reading lists.

Children: The Challenge, by Rudolf Dreikurs and Vicki Soltz. A classic best-seller, excellent on how parents can help children learn from the consequences of their own choices. Published Plume/Penguin ISBN 0-452-26655-6

Parenting Young Children, by Dinkmeyer, McKay and Dinkmeyer. Could be more simply written, but has a wealth of sensible ideas and good examples to illustrate each point the authors make. Published AGS, Circle Pines, Minnesota 55014-1796. ISBN 0-88671-356-0

Play with a Purpose for under-sevens, by Elizabeth Matterson, Another classic, full of wisdom and good sense, and written from wide experience. Interestingly, the author prefers the word 'play' to 'experiential learning' because the word 'play' captures the *fun* that goes with learning. Publ. Penguin Books.

The Heart of Parenting, by John Gottman. The findings of one of the leading research psychologists in the world are made available here in simple language. His studies reveal what works in parenting and what does not work. You will see how the 0-6 Programme reinforces what Gottman calls 'emotional coaching' – how parents speak, listen, encourage, show affection, respect feelings, offer choices and allow children to learn from living with the consequences of their choices. Published Bloomsbury. ISBN 0-7475-3312-1

The Complete Secrets of Happy Children: A Guide for Parents. by Steve and Sharon Biddulph (December 2003). Also **Raising Babies: Why Your Love is Best** (March 2006) and **The Secret of Happy Parents: How to Stay in Love as a Couple and True to Yourself.** (August 2004). The Biddulphs write with humour and simplicity – these are very readable, inspiring and challenging books for parents, easily available online.

What Mothers Do – especially when it looks like nothing, by Naomi Stadlen, is an understanding and reassuring book for any house-parent who wonders, "What have I been doing all day?" Described by the Guardian as 'the best book on parenting.' Published Piatkus (2004) ISBN 0-74992620-1

FURTHER READING ON CHILDREN'S SPIRITUAL GROWTH

It is not easy to find books to help parents nurture their children's spiritual growth – most books on family spirituality deal too much with prayer and not enough with the more grounded spirituality of daily living and loving. The best we have come across were published by Methodist Publishing House in Peterborough – **Praying with sticky fingers**, by Helen Albans, and **Milestones**, by Christine Elliott Hall, Judy Jarvis and Mary Jefferson. Unfortunately, Methodist Publishing House has disappeared and these books are no longer in print, but you may be able to pick them up second-hand online. In the Roman Catholic tradition, <u>**A Community of Love: Spirituality of Family Life**</u> by David M. Thomas (Mar 2007) comes strongly recommended – Acta Publications. ISBN 13:978-0-87946-327-4. We welcome other recommendations.

SOME OF YOUR COMMENTS

All the comments below were made by people attending the Noughts to Sixes course.

• I'm teaching primary two, and I'm shocked at how poor some children are at doing things for themselves – putting on a coat, opening a bottle, anything... And you can see it's the same children whose parents do everything for them when they leave them off or collect them. They mean well, but honestly, I wish they could see what a disadvantage it's creating for their children.

• When they're squabbling, I find a good way of not doing what I normally do is just to 'observe' what's happening without saying anything – that seems to make them aware of what's going on for them and what they really need.

• I lay quietly beside my daughter as she coloured in a picture. I noticed I wanted to correct her. I also wanted to colour in some parts myself, or at least ask adult questions "Why did you colour her lips green?" or make adult suggestions, "Wouldn't you be better to colour this yellow?" Instead, I just noticed her. Then I realised I was bored. I wanted to distract her, or do something else. It's awful, isn't it, that I feel such a compulsion to be 'active,' to take over, to interfere. Anyway, I stayed quiet and watched her and made an occasional comment, "You've coloured all that in." And you know, she picked up that I was interested and not interfering, and she said, "Would you like me to show you the other pictures?"

• My three-year-old clears her plate and cup from the table now. I don't have to remind her. And she's so pleased with herself!

• I don't think it's right to give a small child a choice about wearing his coat on a cold day, but I find he co-operates when I offer him a choice of mittens and old scarves to go with it.

• I noticed David very weepy and depressed for a few days. One lunchtime, I got him on his own and asked what was wrong. "My mummy has no time for me any more since the baby came," he said. "I miss her." He cried. Next day, I told his mother what he had said, thinking she'd be interested, but all she said was, "He'll have to grow up!" I felt so sad for him then.

• When he realised he was losing the game of draughts, he refused to move. Normally, I would have got angry and lectured him that "somebody has to lose, and you should be a sport." But because of the session on listening, I looked at him, and said, "You're feeling sad." He nodded. "Do you want a hug?" I asked. Again he nodded, came around for a hug and cried his little heart out. It wasn't about the draughts – I'll never know what it was about, but he badly needed to cry, and it did him the world of good."

• He came in from play, announced he didn't want dinner, and lay on his bed. I waited a while, then went in, put my arm around him and got him to tell me what was troubling him. I said very little – I think it was my silence got him to talk more. After a while, he said, "I feel better now anyway. I think I'll have my dinner."

• When he asked me if there really was a Santa Claus, I said, "Yes, Santa Claus is real for all the children who believe in him. He's not real if you don't believe in him." He went off contented!

• He refused to get ready for bed. I could see he was full of resistance, so I gave him a choice, "Do you want me to put on your pyjamas, or do you want to do it yourself?" That broke through the resistance a bit. "You do it," he said. He let me undress him (which I know would have been a power struggle if I hadn't given him the choice), but when I went to put on the pyjamas, he became contrary and crossed his legs. "Okay," I said, "you can put on the pyjamas," and I got up to leave. "No, you do it," he said, and he put out his legs." Choices are great – they're respectful and they're effective!

• I heard myself saying, "No, I'm too busy," when he asked me for a piggy-back, and I thought, "What's happening to me? I'd time to carry him everywhere when he was a baby!"

• When my sister was staying for the weekend, my son must have picked up the vibes that she was 'available,' and asked her "will you play a board game with me?" It's sobering – he'd stopped asking *me*!

MAKING AGREEMENTS

It may help to discuss and agree on these and any other points that participants may wish to raise at the beginning of a course.

1. **Take it seriously.** It is suggested that you practise the skills at least once each day during the course and take some time each evening 1) to become aware of how you've been doing, and 2) to imagine how you will act in a situation you will meet the next day. Those who work at the skills between sessions tend to see a great improvement in themselves and in their family life.

2. **No pressure.** You are not expected to agree with everything on the course, and you have a right not to speak at any time. No pressure will be put on you to do anything in the group that you don't want to do.

3. **Encourage others to speak.** You are asked not to speak a second time about any topic until everyone has at least had an *opportunity* to speak once. Hogging the conversation is not fair to others. If you tend to talk a lot, you might draw others out instead, listening to them and encouraging *them* to talk first.

4. **Don't tell me – show me.** Changing yourself is the key to change in your own family – your children, your partner, your parents will usually only begin to change when *you* do. How you *behave* speaks much louder than what you *say*.

5. **Beat discouragement.** As you improve, you will sometimes have a bad day when you seem to go backwards. That is normal – everyone has off-days. But don't let yourself get discouraged or think you have failed if you are slow about changing the habits of a lifetime. *Any* new skill tends to feel strange and awkward to start with.

6. **Take it slowly.** Don't start by tackling situations that are very difficult for you. Better to build up your confidence by practising the skills of this course with small things and easier situations first.

7. **Look out for strengths.** This is a positive, family-building support group, so you are asked not to criticise your children, your partner or others. Please appreciate the efforts, sacrifices and improvements of each parent in the group. Parents are often starved of appreciation for their parenting.

8. **No preaching.** The input for this course comes from the video and the leader's guide – not from the leader. The leader, then, will not be giving you advice. But you are asked to show the same respect to each *other*. You can make suggestions or say what works for *you*, but please speak personally and do not put pressure on others or tell them what to do. They all have a right to their own approach and their own pace. This applies also to a partner who is not doing the course with you – though it may help to discuss the ideas with a partner and to involve them by sharing the book and video with them.

9. **Respect people's confidences.** If it comes to light during a course that a child is at risk because of physical or sexual abuse, there is a legal obligation on us to inform social services. Apart from this exception, it is *very* important to respect confidentiality and not to talk to anyone about what you hear in the group.

10. **Anything else...** that would help you to feel safer in the group?

SUPPORT FOR PARENTING

THE 'NOUGHTS TO SIXES' PARENTING PROGRAMME

Seven or eight weekly sessions offering effective parenting support to parents of babies, toddlers, pre-schoolers or children in the first few years of primary school. Simply written, jargon-free, common sense approach. Produced in co-operation with Barnardos. The boxed kit includes audio-visual input, incorporating the BBC's acclaimed QED programme on parenting (choose either DVD or video format), two leader's guides, twenty-five certificates, and one copy of the parent's handbook, **From Pram to Primary School.**

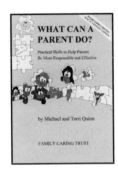

THE 'FIVES TO FIFTEENS' PARENTING PROGRAMME

Eight weekly sessions to help parents of children five to fifteen years old to improve their communication skills and create a framework of discipline and respect in their families. The boxed kit includes about ten minutes' audio-visual input for each session (choose either DVD or video format), two leader's guides, twenty-five certificates, and one copy of the parent's handbook, **What Can A Parent Do?**

THE 'PARENTING TEENAGERS' PROGRAMME

Six to eight weekly sessions to reinforce the same parenting skills while dealing with the more difficult situations met in the teen years. Because it is so important to reinforce skills being learnt, it is recommended that parents of teenagers experience the Fives to Fifteens programme first, though this is not essential. The kit includes audio-visual input (choose either DVD or video format), two leader's guides, twenty-five certificates, and one copy of the parent's handbook, **What Can The Parent Of A Teenager Do?**

THE 'PARENT ASSERTIVENESS' PROGRAMME

Seven weekly sessions learning basic assertive skills applied to the workplace or neighbourhood, but especially to family situations. A good way of complementing what has been learnt in the other parenting programmes. Produced in co-operation with Barnardos. The boxed kit includes audio-visual input (choose either DVD or video format), two leader's guides and one copy of the participant's handbook, **Being Assertive.**

SUPPORT FOR YOUNG ADULTS

THE YOUNG ADULT ASSERTIVENESS PROGRAMME

Eight weekly sessions to help young adults, aged fifteen and upwards, to learn the same respectful skills as their parents and thus reinforce change within the family system. The emphasis is on growth in self-confidence, saying 'no' to peer pressure and finding fairer, less aggressive ways of dealing with problems. The boxed kit includes a video, two leader's guides, a pack of twenty-five certs, and one copy of the participant's handbook, **Taking Charge of your Life.**

SUPPORT FOR COUPLES

THE 'COUPLE ALIVE' PROGRAMME

Six weekly sessions for couples at all stages - engaged, cohabiting, recently married or married up to forty years. Helps couples deepen or renew their love, commitment and understanding for one another. Also teaches the "Listen and Check" method which has reduced rates of separation, divorce and domestic violence in Europe and the United States. This programme is endorsed by co-ordinators from Relate, the Marriage Enrichment Association, and Accord. The boxed kit includes a video, two leader's guides, and a participant's handbook, **Couple Alive.**

The Trust has no links with any religious body, but there is an optional Christian dimension and an optional Islamic dimension for each course, emphasising a family spirituality that is grounded in daily living: they have been written by people belonging to those faiths.

ADDITIONAL RESOURCES

Manual for training people to run Family Caring Trust programmes. A resource to provide an accredited training for facilitators of parenting programmes (accreditation by the Open College Network at Level 3). Developed by Hallam Caring Services in co-operation with people from the Education, Health, Social Services and Voluntary sectors.

Introductory video/DVD 25-min. videocassette (or DVD) useful for information evening or introductory session. Shows effect of the parenting course on two families. Made independently by RTE, and provided at duplication cost.

Leader's CD. CD to help facilitators understand their role and to reinforce skills they need.

For over a decade, Family Caring Trust has been the main provider of parent education in the UK and Ireland. Almost half a million parents in these isles have taken one of these courses. The materials have also been adapted to different cultures and translated into Afrikaans, Arabic, Bengali, Bulgarian, Czech, Danish, Icelandic, Japanese, Latvian, Punjabi, Russian, Somali, Spanish, Sylheti, Tamil, Urdu, Welsh and Xhosa. In addition to being widely used by social services and well over a thousand schools and adult education bodies, they have been adopted or endorsed by the following organisations:

The Health Visitors' Association (CPHVA), Sure Start, Barnardos, The Children's Society, Homestart, The National Childbirth Trust, All the mainstream Christian Churches, NSPCC, Accord, Mothers' Union, The Marriage Enrichment Association, NCH, and the Psychological Services in Scotland.

(Family Caring Trust gratefully acknowledges the contribution of **Barnardos** and the **Department of Health** to the development and production of some of these courses.)